*For Cathri***

With lots

CW00924514

The Author *Richard*

London, July 2018

Photograph by C. Walczyk

David Poole

1926–1991

A life blighted by Apartheid

Richard Glasstone

The Book Guild Ltd

First published in Great Britain in 2018 by
The Book Guild Ltd
9 Priory Business Park
Wistow Road, Kibworth
Leicestershire, LE8 0RX
Freephone: 0800 999 2982
www.bookguild.co.uk
Email: info@bookguild.co.uk
Twitter: @bookguild

Typeset in Aldine401 BT

Printed and bound in Great Britain by CPI Group (UK) Ltd, Croydon, CR0 4YY

ISBN 978 1912575 046

British Library Cataloguing in Publication Data.
A catalogue record for this book is available from the British Library.

Contents

Introduction

The National Party first assumed power following the 1948 South African elections.

Their prime minister, J F Malan, served from 1948 to 1954 and immediately began to implement the notorious *apartheid* laws which Hendrik Verwoerd had advocated.

This is the time line for the implementation of the *apartheid* laws

1949: Prohibition Of Mixed Marriages Act – This made any further marriages between persons of different races strictly illegal.

1950: Immorality Act – This criminalised all sexual relations between the different races.

1950: Population Registration Act – This formalised the racial classification of the entire population into four distinct groups: WHITE, COLOURED, INDIAN or BLACK. In the case of mixed race individuals, special boards were established to decide to which of these four groups each person was to be assigned. Everyone over the age of eighteen was then issued with the relevant Identity Card. This was to have devastating consequences when several members of the same family were allocated to different racial groups, as was to happen in the case of David Poole's family.

1950: Group Areas Act – Whereas previously there had been a number of areas in which people of different races had lived happily side by side, that was now declared to be illegal. Each race was allocated its own, officially designated areas. This often resulted in the enforced removal of recalcitrant individuals or even of whole communities from areas where they had lived for generations.

1953: Reservation Of Separate Amenities Act – This reserved areas of certain amenities, such as beaches, schools, universities, parks, trains and buses, for the use of specific racial groups.

1953: Bantu Education Act – This established separate education systems for black South Africans. In this respect it is often forgotten that, historically, there had been relatively few indigenous black African people living in the Cape Province. However, during World War II, with many white South Africans serving in the Armed Forces, the ensuing shortage of white labour attracted many black migrant workers to a number of economically flourishing urban centres, including many areas of the Cape Province. This was increasingly resented by many of the white Afrikaners of Dutch, German and French Huguenot descent, leading to their espousal of the National Party with its promise that the *apartheid* system it advocated would ensure the continuing dominance of South Africa's white population.

J G Strijdom was to replace J F Malan as Prime Minister of South Africa – he served from 1954 to 1958. His Promotion of Black Self-Government Act was to entrench the National Party's policy of establishing "independent" homelands for the black population. This complex – and ultimately unsuccessful – policy is of less interest in the present context than was Strijdom's success in finally achieving the deplorable removal of the franchise from the Cape Coloured community. Whereas Malan had tried unsuccessfully to deny this mixed-race community their long-held and constitutionally entrenched voting rights, Strijdom now embarked on a series of shamelessly unscrupulous political manoeuvres to achieve his aim.

1

South Africa's Cape Coloured People

The Dutch East India Company founded what was eventually to become Cape Town in order to use it as a re-supply port for ships trading between The Netherlands and the East Indies. In 1652 they dispatched Jan van Riebeek there to establish farms to grow the fruit and vegetables needed to combat the scurvy suffered by sailors during long sea voyages. Cape Town's present-day Company Gardens are still a testament to those times.

When the first white men disembarked at the Cape the indigenous inhabitants they encountered there were the San people, who were hunter-gatherers, and the Khoi, who owned some cattle. The San were soon hunted almost to extinction by the white invaders, whereas the Dutch settlers coerced some of the Khoi into working for them as indentured labourers on the farms, which were now providing fresh produce for the Dutch East India Company's passing ships.

Initially, the settlers were not allowed to be accompanied by their wives, nor were they permitted to own slaves. What the Company had originally set up merely as a trading post soon began to expand into an increasingly prosperous Dutch settler colony. This was becoming a desirable retirement place for a growing number of the Company's employees. They were granted permission to lease land as Vryburgers ("free citizens") and, in return, the crops which they cultivated had to be sold to the Dutch East India Company's ships at a fixed price. As the Vryburgers' farms prospered and began needing larger labour forces, the Company started allowing the settlers to import slaves from Asia as well as from Madagascar and Mozambique.

The presence of increasing numbers of female slaves, combined with the initial absence of any Dutch women, would inevitably lead to the miscegenation that resulted in the vast number of mixed-race men and women who became known as South Africa's Cape Coloured people. They were the descendants of unions between white men and female slaves of mainly Asian origin, as well as of those between Asian or black African male slaves and women of the Cape of Good Hope's indigenous inhabitants, the Khoi and the San peoples. It is estimated that some 60,000 black and Asian slaves were imported either from Madagascar and Mozambique or from the East Indies. Many of these slaves adopted their owners' Calvinist faith, whilst those who came from Indonesia were mainly the Moslems who were later to become known as the Cape Malay community.

Once the Company started allowing the settlers to be accompanied by their wives, these women had to converse with their slaves in a sort of 'kitchen Dutch'. This mixture of basic Dutch with various words used by the slaves in their own languages – such as *piesang* for banana, *piering* meaning saucer and *blatjang* for chutney – eventually morphed into the simple form of Afrikaans which, with the later addition of many English expressions, is still the language spoken by most of the Cape Coloured people.

Among themselves, the settlers spoke in High Dutch rather than in Afrikaans, which they despised as a mongrel language.

Gradually, with the influx of Germans and French Huguenots, the original settlers were becoming a rather amorphous group, in need of finding some sort of unity. There is a somewhat contentious theory that this was to develop into the so-called "Myth of the Afrikaner Nation". The Dutch grammarians among them started defining the principles of what was to evolve into 'respectable' Afrikaans. They had to 'invent' some history and saw Jan van Riebeek as the divinely inspired forefather of the Afrikaner Nation. A theory many Afrikaners will probably dispute!

It is interesting to note that the first book to be published in Afrikaans was the Koran, transliterated into Arabic script. It had been the slaves imported from Indonesia who were the first people in South Africa to practise the Moslem faith. In later years, once slavery had been abolished, a very warm, friendly and devout community of Moslems flourished in what became known as Cape Town's Malay Quarter. Before the advent of the National Party and its *apartheid* laws, Cape Town's District Six was home to a colourful and dynamic mixed-race community, boasting several mosques as well as a number of Jewish synagogues. Indeed, until the notorious Group Areas Act was implemented, both communities lived there happily side by side. As a young student teacher, I taught ballet in District Six, at the Eoan Group, to teenagers of all races. I also enjoyed eating in a particular District Six restaurant, famous for its delicious *samosas* and Cape Malay curry with *blatjang*.

In recent years, in Barrydale, a little town several hours' drive from Cape Town, a wonderfully dynamic organisation called "*Net vir Pret*" ("Just for Fun") has been doing important work among that area's large Cape Coloured community. Under the enlightened guidance of Derek Joubert and his team of devoted helpers, this largely impoverished and deprived community has been very successfully introduced to a wide variety of Arts and Education programmes. These culminate each year in a themed Christmas Parade, involving acting, singing, dancing and wonderfully imaginative puppetry. The theme for one of these events was the history of South Africa's slave trade. In the process of researching that history, Derek was astonished to discover how little the local Coloured people knew about this subject. These Afrikaans-speaking descendants of earlier unions between slaves from various countries and the indigenous Khoi and San people were initially reluctant to accept that as fact. *"Ek is nie Khoi nie, ek is kleurling"* ("I am not Khoi, I am Coloured") was a frequent response. However, once these people had begun to understand and appreciate their own history, the touching reaction expressed by one of them was: "I used to think I was a Cape Coloured, and that was that; but now I know that I have Khoi and slave blood, I feel very rich and proud."

All the illustrations in this Chapter are courtesy of Net vir Pret and Derek Joubert.

The giant Ostrich was made by Handspring Puppets
for the 2012 Christmas Parade.

The giant Elephant was made by Handspring Puppets
for the 2013 Christmas Parade.

The giant Eiland was made by Handspring Puppets
for the 2014 Christmas Parade.

Chriswn in the pottery studio, admiring the chimes
he has been making.

A crowded reading class with some of the
enthusiastic younger children.

Girls in the homework room, working on
an educational programme.

Showing off objects made from rubbish collected
when cleaning up the village.

Young lad practising the guitar, surrounded by
lots of reading matter.

A child wearing a giraffe head, made in the
Net vir Pret puppet workshop.

2

David Poole and Johaar Mosaval

David Poole was studying at Zonnebloem College during the early 1940s, training to be a schoolteacher. This was at a Cape Coloured institution situated in District Six, a mixed-race area in the heart of Cape Town. One day, he was sent as a supply teacher to the George Ashley Golding Primary School – another of District Six's Cape Coloured educational premises. One of the pupils at this school was a young Moslem boy called Johaar Mosaval.

A year or two earlier, Johaar had started showing an enthusiastic interest in ballet. This was brought to the attention of Jasmine Honoré, a talented dancer who had trained under Dulcie Howes at the ballet school attached to the University of Cape Town (UCT). Hearing that Johaar seemed to be showing natural dance ability, Jasmine offered to give the young boy his first ballet lessons.

During his secondment to the George Ashley Golding Primary School, David Poole (who had also recently started studying ballet with Dulcie Howes) happened to ask young Johaar what he would like to become. To his surprise, the boy exclaimed: "Oh Sir, one day I am going to be a famous ballet

14

dancer!" David Poole's response was to burst out laughing at what he considered to be the boy's totally unrealistic ambition! There still was a generally harmonious state of co-existence between white South Africans and the Cape Coloured population, with several young Coloured men starting to show an interest in ballet. They were attending classes with Dulcie Howes and Cecily Robinson at UCT, a University with a long-standing liberal tradition. It was therefore quite natural for some Cape Coloured students to be performing with the University Ballet Company. (Unlike people of mixed race, the black population still played little or no part in South Africa's cultural life at that time.) It was, of course, still the case that, throughout the world, those dancers employed by professional ballet companies were almost exclusively white – hence David Poole's negative reaction to Johaar's stated ambition.

In 1995, when I was researching my biography of Dulcie Howes, Johaar told me about an incident which had happened when the young boy's art teacher had taken him to see a ballet performance at the Cape Town City Hall (one of the few public venues not yet operating a colour bar). The programme that evening was presented by the Cape Town Ballet Club and included many dancers from the University Ballet School. When the curtain rose, Johaar thought that one of the dancers looked familiar. "Sir," he whispered to his teacher, "isn't that Mr Poole, who taught at our school last year?" Checking the printed programme, the art master confirmed that it was indeed David Poole. "But Sir," exclaimed the boy, "he's dancing with white girls!" Pressing a finger firmly to his lips, the teacher cautioned silence and discretion. It is against this sort of background that one must consider Dulcie Howes's involvement with Cape Town's non-white community.

Meanwhile, David Poole was continuing to make rapid progress and was starting to develop into a promising expressive dancer. As well as performing with the University Ballet and the Cape Town Ballet Club, he was also dancing with the Eoan Group. That organisation had been founded in 1933 by Mrs Helen Southern-Holt, who was very involved in community work with the Cape Coloured people. With the help of her daughter, Dr Mary Southern-Holt, she oversaw the development of the Eoan Group from its humble beginnings in a small room in District Six to a large and flourishing organisation, encompassing ballet, drama, music, opera and various other educational and cultural activities. The staging of a 'Masque of Nymphs and Reapers' as part of a performance of *The Tempest,* as devised by Dulcie Howes, using a non-white cast including David Poole, was but one of several examples of the close co-operation between the University Ballet and the Eoan Group.

In 1945, John Cranko, a young white youth from Johannesburg then still in his late teens, also started studying ballet with Dulcie Howes, at Cape Town University. He was eventually destined to become that school's most famous alumnus and, as a choreographer, Cranko was later to enjoy a distinguished international career. Now, within months of arriving in Cape Town, he created his first ballet *The Soldier's Tale* to Stravinsky's score. David Poole danced the title role, partnering another of Dulcie Howes's students, Pamela Chrimes – one more example of a Cape Coloured man dancing with a young white woman. Was it perhaps Poole's success in Cranko's first ballet that convinced Dulcie Howes that the time was right for David to continue his training in London? As can be gauged from the following letter, addressed to Howes by the Director of England's Sadler's Wells Ballet, Ninette de Valois, it appears that South African dancers were indeed starting to gain a fine reputation abroad.

On the 4th of June 1946, Ninette de Valois wrote:

"My dear Dulcie, Of course I will give your pupil a scholarship and, from all accounts, he will be in one or other of the companies pretty quickly; but as you say, in all fairness to the Management, I must see him dance first. If he is very talented and it is a question of letting him shake down in the school for a couple of months before we use him, he would no doubt be entitled to our further scholarship scheme for young men: a maintenance grant amounting to about two pounds a week towards his keep during his study time. But get him over here first and you can rest assured I will do all I can. With regard to his passage, if we can help in any way by saying we have granted him a scholarship to study with a view to joining the English ballet, please let me know if I can do anything at this end. I am grateful to you for letting me know about him. I assure you that our aim, now that we are developing, is to draw our male dancers from Australia, South Africa and Canada; in fact, I want to give all the Colonies and Dominions preference over foreign dancers entering the Sadler's Wells Ballet; so please help all you can. When you hear of talent, I will see it. Pamela Chrimes is already doing very well in the second company.

Hoping to see you as soon as possible, Yours sincerely, Ninette de Valois."

There has been a certain amount of speculation as to whether the un-named pupil in this letter was John Cranko or David Poole? In fact, Cranko had already sailed for Europe several months before this letter was written, and his immense choreographic talent was very soon recognised by Ninette de Valois. It was not until the following year, in 1947, that arrangements were finally made for David Poole to travel to London to study briefly at the Sadler's Wells School, prior to starting what was to become his lengthy and immensely successful career, dancing with the Sadler's Wells Theatre Ballet Company.

But what was happening to Johaar Mosaval? In 1947, not long after his 18th birthday, it was going to be his turn to travel to London. For the previous two years he had been continuing his ballet training with Dulcie Howes at the University Ballet School. As the son of devout Moslem parents, Johaar had had to combat a certain amount of family opposition to the notion of his wanting to become a professional ballet dancer. However, Dulcie Howes became increasingly convinced of this young man's distinctive talent and she championed his cause, urging his family to support and encourage him as much as possible. But how practical were Johaar's chances of being able to realise his boyhood dream of becoming "a famous ballet dancer"?

In 1948 the National Party had come to power and had soon started implementing a number of very divisive *apartheid* laws. One of these laws – the 1950 Population Registration Act – formalised the division of the entire population into one of four distinct racial groups. Moreover, whereas there had also been a few areas – such as Cape Town's District Six – where people of different races had been living happily side by side for generations, this was now made illegal by another law issued that same year, the Group Areas Act. That resulted in the break-up of entire communities and their enforced removal to separate racially-segregated residential areas. The opportunities which Cape Town University had provided for white and mixed-race dancers to study and perform together were soon to be made illegal by the implementation of the Reservation of Separate Amenities Act. That would make it impossible for Johaar to be able to realise his boyhood dream in South Africa.

In 1951, a fund was set up to finance the cost of Mosaval's travel to England to enrol at the Sadler's Wells School where – as had been the case with both Cranko and Poole – his talent was soon recognised, leading to his joining the *corps de ballet* of the Sadler's Wells Ballet Company. He was later made a soloist and was then promoted to the status of Principal Dancer, performing at the Sadler's Wells Theatre as well as with the Royal Ballet Company at Covent Garden.

In 1954, the Sadler's Wells Theatre Ballet embarked on a

much-publicised tour of South Africa. David Poole was by then one of that Company's leading dancers. I was in my final year at UCT, and I still have vivid memories of David's wonderfully expressive performances in ballets such as Cranko's *Pineapple Poll,* as well as in *Blood Wedding*, a ballet by another South African choreographer and UCT alumnus, Alfred Rodrigues. But it was not until the following year, when I too travelled to England, that I was able to see Johaar dance. He had NOT been allowed to travel to South Africa with the other members of the Company. Whereas Poole was able to be passed off as white, Mosaval was too dark-skinned to be allowed to perform in South Africa's theatres which, by then, were all operating a strict colour bar.

Two important points need to be made in this connection: Firstly, that a British ballet company was prepared to go along with South Africa's *apartheid* laws, compelling it to leave Mosaval behind. This, of course, was before the trade union Equity had begun to bar British artists from performing in South Africa. I make no value judgements as to the rights and wrongs of this whole, complex situation; but the fact that cultural links with Europe were still flourishing was naturally of enormous artistic importance to the South Africans. The second point to stress in this Poole/Mosaval controversy is an ironic and paradoxical one. These two non-white dancers had been trained largely in a white ballet school and had been able to dance with white girls *in South Africa itself!* This was because, at that time, those performances took place in the Little Theatre on the UCT campus, or at the City Hall, belonging to a liberal municipality which held out for as long as possible against the Central Government's *apartheid* legislation.

Even before the implementation of the National Party's *apartheid* laws, racial segregation had been more a matter of tacit social convention than one of law. There undoubtedly existed an unspoken 'hierarchy of pigmentation' which enabled the lighter-skinned Cape Coloureds to fare better than those of a darker hue. The degree of discrimination encountered by non-whites was also affected by other criteria, such as individual levels of education and personal economic circumstances, as well as by that nebulous but potent factor, social class. During the 1950s, when I was a student in Cape Town, there was still a considerable degree of co-operation between the white and the Cape Coloured communities – in particular in the Arts. At times this was on a truly non-racial basis; in other instances (notably with regard to that somewhat contentious organisation, the Eoan Group) it was a case of white teachers and producers directing exclusively non-white cultural activities.

The Eoan Group certainly did a great deal to nurture the talents of many mixed-race young people; yet, with hindsight, one now realises that it also played a part in perpetuating the disadvantaged status of the very people it was intended to serve. In South Africa – as in many other parts of the world – the British had spread their cultural and moral values through their language and via various cultural institutions, as well as through the Church. They then often proceeded to erect barriers to protect their own racial exclusivity. Founded by two well-meaning English women, the Eoan Group could perhaps be said to have inadvertently helped to keep the Cape Coloured people safely in their own racial ghetto.

'Masque of Nymphs and Reapers' devised by Dulcie Howes for a staging of The Tempest in 1946, with a non-white cast of the UCT Ballet School's male students. David Poole is reclining in the foreground. The girls appeared by courtesy of The Eoan Group. *Photo – Constance Stuart.*

David Poole in Dulcie Howes's ballet St Valentine's Eve, circa 1943.

Photo – John Barnes.

David Poole and Pamela Chrimes in Cranko's The Soldier's Tale in 1945.

Photo – Anne Fisher.

David Poole with Richard Glasstone (above) in the University Ballet
Company's staging of Ninette de Valois' ballet The Haunted Ballroom in
the early 1960s. *Photo – John Reader.*

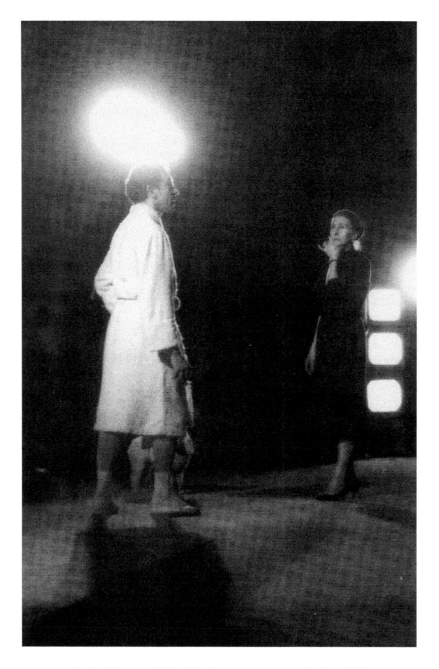

Dulcie Howes and David Poole at a stage rehearsal, circa 1969.
Photo – Victor Glasstone.

Basil Poole (David's younger brother) as Captain Belaye, with UCT
students in the University Ballet Company's staging of John Cranko's
Pineapple Poll in the mid-1960s. *Photo – Charles Field.*

3

Two Different Types of Apartheid Law

"Grand Apartheid" included laws such as the Population Registration Act – this formalised the classification of the population into four distinct racial groups: White, Coloured, Indian or Black. The Group Areas Act allocated separate, officially designated living areas to each of these four racial groups. This often resulted in the enforced removal and resettlement of whole communities.

"Petty Apartheid" included measures such as the Reservation of Separate Amenities Act which reserved certain amenities, such as parts of beaches, parks, train carriages or parts of buses for the exclusive use of specific racial groups.

My friend Derek recalls a typical example of "petty apartheid" which had occurred when, as a white teacher working temporarily in a Coloured school, he boarded a bus with a group of his pupils and joined them on the upper deck, which was reserved for non-white passengers. The bus conductor ordered Derek to go down to the lower deck, reserved for white passengers, and obstinately refused to allow the bus driver to proceed until each racial group was seated in its specifically allocated area.

I too recall – with a combination of disgust and incredulity – the fact that, when buying my newspaper each morning from a suburban railway station's tiny bookstall, I was compelled to do so by standing on the correct side of the small barrier separating white from non-white customers!

A typical example of how one could find oneself the victim of a combination of both "Grand" and "Petty" *apartheid* befell Len Martin, my fellow-student at UCT. Because he had been registered as Coloured, he could not be served at the little Rondebosch café where we white students bought our lunch; so, I would offer to purchase something for him to eat. When Len and I walked down together to the railway station, we had to buy our tickets from separate windows before boarding separate train carriages. I never did get to see where Len lived, as his family had been forcibly moved to a Coloured area. Yet, at that time, this brilliant young dancer was performing the lead role of Harlequin in a white university's staging of Fokine's *Carnaval*. Our Director, Dulcie Howes, was somehow managing to observe *apartheid* regulations by skirting them!

One of the weirdest anomalies of *apartheid* legislation was that whilst the Chinese were classified as 'coloured' the Japanese, because of the South African government's important economic ties with Japan, were granted the status of 'honorary whites.' This enabled visiting Japanese businessmen to use 'whites only' hotels and restaurants. In 1961, when Heather Magoon was a student at the UCT's Michaelis Art School, there was a Chinese youth in her year called Denis Ah Chong. At that same time, I was teaching his sister Helen at the Eoan Group. Arriving at Art School one morning, Heather was surprised to find Denis sitting outside the Life Drawing class. Although the Art School generally employed non-white models, that morning the model was a white woman and she objected to having Denis in the class. She clearly thought that she had the right to exclude this Chinese youth!

Apartheid and the Church

The separate development of South Africa's racial groups, advocated by the government, was also supported by the Dutch Reformed Church, which sought to justify *apartheid* on biblical grounds. There was a small group of dissenters – among them the Afrikaner Professor B. B. Keet – whose thoughtful and cogently argued little book *Suid-Africa – Waarheen?* ("Whither South Africa?") cites the bible in Paul, Acts 17:26: *"God het uit een bloed al die nasies van die mensdom gemaak om oor die hele aarde te woon"* ("God made from one blood all the nations of men to dwell on the face of the earth"). Professor Keet was one of a small number of Afrikaner Academics and Theologians who had begun to have their doubts regarding the Dutch Reformed Church's justification of *apartheid*. One of the most prominent of these dissenters was C. T. Beyers Naudé.

Beyers Naudé had studied theology at Stellenbosch University where his sociology lecturer was the chief proponent of *apartheid*, H. F. Verwoerd, a long-standing member of the *Broederbond* ("The Brotherhood"), a secret society dedicated to the advancement of the Afrikaner people. This organisation, whose origins dated back to before the 1920s, exerted enormous influence on all aspects of South Africa's political and social life. After graduating from Stellenbosch University, Beyers Naudé was ordained as a *Dominee* (a Minister) of the Dutch Reformed Church in 1939. He was also admitted to the *Broederbond* as its youngest member. For some twenty years, Naudé remained a loyal member of his Church, ministering to a variety of congregations. But the violence of the 1960 Sharpeville massacre finally shattered his faith in the *apartheid* system.

This was the notorious event in which a large group of black men demonstrating against a series of laws restricting their freedom of movement was randomly fired on by the police, killing 69 of the protestors. This was to lead Naudé to start questioning the validity of the Church's so-called biblical justification for the *apartheid* system. He undertook an exhaustive search of the bible, but was unable to find any really convincing justification for the Church's stance.

As he became more and more outspoken, he inevitably aroused fierce opposition from both the Government and the Church. In 1963, Beyers Naudé founded the Christian Institute of Southern Africa, an ecumenical organisation fostering reconciliation through interracial dialogue. Both the Church and the Government were implacably opposed to the activities of Naudé and his fellow-dissenters in the Christian Institute, placing every possible impediment in their way. Eventually, the Dutch Reformed Church forced Naudé to choose between his status as a *Dominee* and his post as the director of the Christian Institute. His response was to resign from both his ministry and from the *Broederbond*. In his last sermon to his congregation he is reported to have declared that "We must show greater loyalty to God than to man".

In 1977 he was sentenced to detention under the harsh restrictions of the system of 'house arrest' and was not released until 1984. In spite of being under constant police surveillance, Naudé was somehow able to help several other fellow-dissenters to move around and out of South Africa. After his own release from detention, Beyers Naudé succeeded the Anglican Archbishop, Desmond Tutu, as Secretary General of the South African Council of Churches which, unlike the Dutch Reformed Church, was increasingly critical of *apartheid*. In 1990, Naudé's uniquely stoic resistance to the evils of *apartheid* was recognised by the African National Congress in their invitation to him to be the only Afrikaner to join in their negotiations with the National Party, leading eventually to the release of Nelson Mandela and the dawn of the New South Africa.

A somewhat different attitude is reflected in an event related to me by Derek Joubert, who had been running Cape Town's Community Arts Project. This was an organisation which provided tuition in the Arts for people barred from other institutions because of their racial labels, enabling them to meet and interact with others who had similar interests and abilities. Sadly, in 1978, the Arts Project had been given notice to vacate its premises, and Derek managed to find a Coloured school on the edge of District Six which was closing down. That school's Principal assured him that he knew of no new plans for this building, which belonged to the Anglican Church. Accompanied by one of the Centre's trustees, David Poole (who had recently been made Cape Town University's first Professor of Ballet), Derek made an appointment to see Archbishop Russell to seek permission for the Arts Project to rent the now-vacant school building.

The Archdeacon responsible for the administration of the business affairs of the Anglican Church was also present at that meeting. Unfortunately, he resolutely refused to lease the vacant school premises to the Community Arts Project. Professor Poole then became very voluble, appealing to Archbishop Russell to relent. "Why would the Church *not* support an organisation working to help oppressed and deprived people?" demanded Poole. The Archdeacon's response horrified both Derek and Professor Poole: "Gentlemen, you misunderstand the *role* of the Church. We are here to encourage individuals to save their souls, and *not* to engage in charity work!" "I have never in my life heard anything more outrageous!" was Professor Poole's indignant response, as he and Derek stormed out of the Archbishop's office. A few days later, at a matinee performance at the local cinema, Derek bumped into the Archbishop and his wife. They were both looking very relaxed and the cleric wasn't wearing his official 'dog collar'. "Don't worry, Derek," he said. "I'll make sure the Community Arts Project gets the building." A happy ending to an unfortunate affair!

4

The Sadler's Wells Theatre Ballet

Sir Peter Wright, who was for many years the Artistic Director of the Birmingham Royal Ballet, as well as being internationally renowned for his new productions of several of the major 19th century classical ballets, had begun his own career as a professional dancer with the Sadler's Wells Theatre Ballet soon after David Poole had himself arrived from South Africa to join that Company (the SWTB).

My decision to write this biography of David Poole was triggered by a fascinating interview I had with Sir Peter at his London apartment on the 26th of January, 2017. Having seen both Poole and Wright dancing important roles with the SWTB when that Company toured South Africa in 1954, I was now eager to find out more about their early careers. Although Sir Peter had recently celebrated his 90th birthday, he was in good health and his recollections of working with David in the late 1940s and early 1950s were still remarkably clear. He was delighted to hear that I was thinking of writing a book about David – they had been good friends and colleagues and Sir Peter generously offered to answer all my questions. Bearing in mind all the problems so many dancers had faced under South Africa's notorious *apartheid* regime, I began by asking Sir Peter about that particular aspect of David's career with the Sadler's Wells Theatre Ballet. "We never thought of David as a 'coloured man'," Sir Peter assured me, "to us he was just another dancer."

Sir Peter then started to describe David's dancing: "He was certainly no great technician – we had both started studying classical ballet too late in life for that. But David was a remarkable expressive character artist, absolutely unforgettable as Jasper, the lovelorn potboy in John Cranko's *Pineapple Poll*. In another Cranko ballet, *Sea Change*, Poole's performance as the skipper of a fishing vessel who has to break the news to a fisherman's wife that her husband has been lost at sea, David had a way of fixing his gaze on the bereaved young widow that held the audience spellbound."

I can certainly attest to this because, when I was still a student at UCT, David had staged *Sea Change* for the UCT Ballet Company, and I still have a clear picture of how he interacted with the wonderful Jasmine Honoré in the role of the young widow, with that spellbinding fixed gaze described to me so clearly by Sir Peter, some fifty years later! When the SWTB toured South Africa in 1954, I witnessed another unforgettable performance by David Poole in *Blood Wedding,* a ballet choreographed by another UCT alumnus, Alfred Rodrigues. Based on Garcia Lorca's *Bodas de sangre*, it tells the story of how, on the eve of her wedding to a man she does not love, the young bride-to-be escapes into the woods with her lover. David Poole's smouldering performance as the lover, and the subsequent fight in which the lover and the jilted bridegroom kill each other, remains etched on my memory.

"The other great thing about David was that he was a really superb partner," Sir Peter now went on to say. "All the women in our Company longed to be cast in any role in which they would be partnered by him. In Cranko's *The*

Lady and the Fool (which I had also seen during the SWTB's visit to Cape Town) Cranko's complex *pas de deux* sequences with La Capricciosa were a real challenge to David and me, in our roles as two of her suitors. She, of course, prefers the company of two shabby clowns, Moondog and Bootface, in front of whom she sheds her mask, revealing herself as a disillusioned young socialite."

Sir Peter then spoke to me about his enormous respect for Poole's talent as a Ballet Master. "He was a great help to me in a number of roles in which I had been cast as his understudy. In particular, he coached me with great attention to detail in the difficult role of The Man with the Rope in the bedlam scene in *The Rake's Progress*, insisting on my giving it my full energy throughout each rehearsal session. With this, as with every other role that we tackled together, he always stressed the musical aspect, insisting that *you have to BE the music*."

David also played an important role as the dancers' unofficial, but greatly valued, spokesman. This was an aspect of David's contribution to the SWTB which was also corroborated in my discussions with the Company's ballet mistress, Barbara Fewster, when she and I discussed the Sadler's Wells Theatre Ballet's extended tour of Canada and the USA.

Under the management of the Impresario Sol Hurok, this utterly exhausting tour lasted from October 1951 to April 1952. The Director of the SWTB, Ninette de Valois, had agreed that for the duration of that tour, Peggy van Praagh's usual title of Ballet Mistress would be upgraded to that of Assistant Director. Van Praagh had insisted that she needed to have the authority implicit in that new title in view of the onerous responsibilities involved in undertaking a six-month tour with many very young dancers. Two of those dancers were indeed still so young that they were required to have a chaperone accompany them when they reported to the police station in each new city to obtain the necessary clearance for such under-aged young girls to be allowed to perform with the adult members of the Company.

The repertoire for that tour included a number of ballets by Ashton, de Valois and Cranko, the full-length, 3 acts of *Coppélia*, and the second act of *Swan Lake,* as well as Ashton's re-choreographed versions of some of the dances in the last act of *The Nutcracker*. The principal dancers were Elaine Fifield, David Blair and Svetlana Beriosova, whilst David Poole, Patricia Miller and Maryon Lane – all three of them South Africans – were among the soloists performing important roles in several of those ballets. (Johaar Mosaval was not due to arrive from Cape Town to join the SWTB until later on in that year.) Given the problems which were still prevalent, in those days, with regard to race relations in particular parts of the USA (admittedly different from South Africa's rigid *apartheid* regime), it is interesting to speculate as to whether or not Johaar would have been barred from travelling to the USA with the Company, as he was going to be for their South African tour in 1954.

The Company were scheduled to perform in over thirty major cities and many smaller towns, from Quebec to Montreal and San Francisco to Dallas, and culminating in a two-week season in New York. It was 3 o'clock in the morning of the 23rd of March when the Company finally arrived in New York. Ninette de Valois arrived the next day and decided to watch the dancers in their morning class. After their six-month trek across Canada and the USA, the dancers were absolutely exhausted. When de Valois expressed her displeasure with the state of the Company, both in class and in the following rehearsals, David Poole stood up for his colleagues, pointing out to de Valois that they had only just arrived in New York after a really gruelling tour! De Valois was absolutely furious and flatly refused to accept this as an explanation. Tears ensued as the irate de Valois proceeded ruthlessly to change some of the casting, replacing several of the dancers in a number of different roles. Years later, when I told Dame Monica Mason about all of this, she said that, in spite of Madam's many great qualities as a Director, "… that incident was typical of de Valois' unreasonable side."

I was particularly intrigued by a story Sir Peter told me concerning David's interest in the occult. "One day, Patricia Miller, Pirmin Trecu, David Poole and I, feeling rather bored on a wet Sunday afternoon at one or other English seaside resort, decided, just for fun, to consult a local Spiritualist. We were all holding hands in a circle in her darkened salon whilst the Medium went into a trance. We had been warned that we would need to wait until a new spirit was ready to get through to her. Eventually, a voice told us that she had a message for a Spanish person." (This could only have been Pirmin – although he certainly spoke Spanish, he was actually very proud of his Basque heritage.) "We all giggled and probably thought that this could have been a 'set-up', and that the Medium had somehow found out beforehand that Pirmin was supposedly Spanish. The next spirit's message seemed to be directed at Patty Miller: 'I am Jack,' it said, 'and I want to tell you not to worry about me.' Patty said that she knew nobody called Jack, so we laughed that off too. However, six months later, Patty had a letter from her mother in South Africa saying that her long-lost uncle had been killed in a motorcar accident. Patty had never met him and was totally unaware that he was actually called Jack!"

Sir Peter now elaborated on this occult theme, but in a way that was less relevant to David than it was to Johaar: "In Cape Town we met Johaar's parents. They were obviously very upset that their son had NOT been allowed to travel with us to South Africa but, wanting to do something to welcome us to their hometown, they invited some of the dancers to accompany them to a Khalifa, a sort of occult, quasi-religious ceremony, practised among the descendants of the slaves from Indonesia, who – like Johaar's family – were mainly Moslem, and who became known as the Cape Malays.

"We watched in amazement as a group of men took it in turns to walk barefoot over hot coals without flinching – they were clearly in some sort of self-inflicted trance. What followed was certainly not for the squeamish! I watched with mounting disbelief as one after the other of these men proceeded to pierce either his cheeks or his lips with a skewer. Egged on by the assembled observers, they seemed not to feel any pain or discomfort. Many of the older men were clearly very experienced in the practice of these rituals and it was only one of the youngest ones – probably a novice – who seemed to bleed a little. The whole experience was both fascinating and disturbing and certainly a long way from our genteel little spiritualist's séance at the English seaside!"

Needless to say, it had been wonderful for me to find out, at first hand from Sir Peter, so much about David Poole's early days in the Sadler's Wells Theatre Ballet. I had initially admired Poole's superb dramatic performances when I was still a student and he was already a consummate artist, touring South Africa with the SWTB. Then, a decade later, we were both dancing with the CAPAB (Cape Performing Arts Board) Ballet Company; and I even got to understudy him as *Petrushka*. Still later, when he had succeeded Dulcie Howes as Director of CAPAB Ballet, David invited me to choreograph several pieces for that Company and, as well as being colleagues, we became firm friends. But before I get to that part of this story, I want to look at what David did in Europe after leaving the SWTB in 1956.

Pirmin Trecu, Annette Page, Peter Wright, John Copley and David
Poole on tour with the Sadler's Wells Theatre Ballet in the early 1950s.
Photo courtesy of Sir Peter Wright.

The SWTB with David Poole standing in the foreground and Ninette de Valois third from left in the second row.

Photo courtesy of Barbara Fewster OBE.

Johaar Mosaval as Puck in Ashton's The Dream with The Royal Ballet in 1958. *Photo – Roy Round*

David Poole and Patricia Miller in Alfred Rodrigues' "Blood Wedding"
Photo Denis Marney

A young man piercing his body with a sword at a Khalifa.

Photo – Victor Glasstone

David Poole as The Rake in The Rake's Progress.
Photo – Brian Astbury

5

Poole and Mosaval *after* the SWTB

Following very successful careers with the Sadler's Wells Theatre Ballet, during which time David Poole and Johaar Mosaval both rose to the rank of Principal Dancer with that Company, they eventually transferred to the larger Company which was now resident at the Royal Opera House in Covent Garden and was to be renamed The Royal Ballet when the Sadler's Wells Ballet was granted a Royal Charter on the 31st of October, 1956. However, the future careers of these two talented South African dancers would soon be destined to follow very different paths.

Johaar was to remain with the Royal Ballet until 1976, performing with great acclaim in roles as diverse as Bootface, the smaller of the two shabby clowns in *The Lady and the Fool* and Jasper, the lovelorn potboy in *Pineapple Poll* – two ballets choreographed by his fellow South African and UCT alumnus, John Cranko. Johaar also danced the virtuoso role of the Blue Boy in Ashton's *Les Patineurs*, as well as displaying that rare combination of an impeccable classical ballet technique and the subtle sense of humour required in roles such as The Dancing Master in Ninette de Valois' *The Rake's Progress* and Puck in *The Dream*, Frederick Ashton's enchanting balletic interpretation of Shakespeare's *A Midsummer Night's Dream.* Finally, after spending some twenty-five years in England, Mosavaal returned to his native Cape Town where, as we will see, his career and that of David Poole were to combine in following a new direction.

David Poole had been in his element with the SWTB where the repertory was particularly suited to his natural expressiveness and his fine sense of drama. David and his fellow South African John Cranko had joined the SWTB in the same year and, in a number of new works that Cranko choreographed for the SWTB, including *Beauty and the Beast* and *Harlequin in April*, as well as the hugely successful *Pineapple Poll*, both men were able to repeat the close working relationship they had enjoyed back in Cape Town when Cranko had created his first ballet, *The Soldier's Tale,* with David in the title role. It would not be an exaggeration to state that the opportunities which de Valois gave Cranko to create a number of new works using fellow South Africans like Poole, Patricia Miller and Maryon Lane were to play a formative role in the artistic development of the then still young SWTB. But when he transferred to the larger Company at The Royal Opera House, David felt somehow out of place. He was also keen to explore other aspects of dance, both in the UK and in Europe. In 1956, he resigned from the Royal Ballet and applied to audition for the Ballet Rambert.

Any such audition – indeed, if there had actually been one – would have been a mere formality. Marie Rambert had been a great admirer of David's work with the SWTB, and especially of the close creative collaboration between him and John Cranko. 'Mim', as Marie Rambert was affectionately known, had already persuaded Cranko to create a new work for her Company in 1954: *Variations on a Theme,* set to Britten's variations on a theme by Frank Bridge. Madame Rambert was known for her passionate interest in new choreography, as well as for her erudition and her deep understanding of music and literature. Poole would, of course, have been interested in questioning her about her collaboration with Vaslav Nijinsky. (Rambert was a specialist in Dalcroze Eurhythmics and had been asked by Diaghilev to help Nijinsky understand the complex rhythms of Stravinsky's revolutionary score for *The Rite of Spring*.) It was therefore understandable that Poole – a highly intelligent man – wanted to seek pastures new by leaving the Royal Ballet to join the Ballet Rambert.

There was another side to Madame Rambert's personality, and one which I had experienced myself as a student at her school when I first arrived in England: she had a tendency to want to 'mould' any dancer in whom she was particularly interested into some ideal image she had of what that dancer could become. Somewhat perversely, given her passionate interest in innovative ideas, she apparently got it into her head that she could 'mould' David Poole into a different type of dancer. Having started studying ballet rather late in life, David's classical technique was rather limited; but his exceptional ability to convey in movement, mime and body language the innermost feelings of any character he was called upon to play may have convinced Madame Rambert that, by strengthening his ballet technique and combining it with his natural expressive qualities, she could perhaps 'mould' him into the perfect *danseur noble*?

The Ballet Rambert's repertoire already included a very fine version of *Giselle*, as well as Fokine's *Les Sylphides*. Then, in the early 1950s, Madame Rambert decided to fulfil one of her long-term ambitions by adding the 19th Century two-act ballet *La Sylphide* to her Company's repertoire. The manner in which she went about acquiring a particularly fine version of this 19th Century masterpiece is amusingly described in Rambert's autobiography, *Quicksilver*. (*La Sylphide* had been Fokine's initial inspiration for his one-act *Chopiniana*, later re-named *Les Sylphides.)* Although I did not see the Ballet Rambert's staging of *La Sylphide*, it seems likely that Madame Rambert would have had David Poole in mind as someone she could 'mould' into the ideal James – the tragic hero of that ballet – or, indeed, the perfect Albrecht for her re-staging of *Giselle*? Be that as it may, David Poole's association with the Ballet Rambert lasted little more than one year. He was now tempted to accept an offer to teach ballet in Germany, at Kurt Jooss's famous Folkwang School in Essen, in 1957.

Kurt Jooss was one of the first choreographers to attempt a synthesis of classical ballet and modern dance techniques. His finest work, *The Green Table*, was a satire inspired by the First World War. Politicians are seen meeting at a conference around the eponymous 'green table' to decide the fate of mankind. David Poole would have been attracted by the opportunity to observe Jooss's work in Germany and to acquire a greater understanding of some of the various Central European styles of movement. He was to become passionately interested in the concept of using theatrical dance to express contemporary ideas, and this would later inspire much of his own choreography when he later returned to his native South Africa. Before that, he was to appear in one more major dance role in Europe: performing at that year's Edinburgh Festival.

The Edinburgh International Company was formed by Peggy van Praagh for the 1958 Edinburgh Festival to display new work choreographed by, among others, John Cranko, Birgit Cullberg and Alan Carter. These ballets were performed by an array of well-known dancers, such as Carla Fracci, Marjorie Tallchief, George Skibine and David Poole. This specially formed Company's most notable production was Walter Gore's extraordinarily moving ballet *The Night and the Silence*. Danced by David Poole and Paula Hinton this work dramatised, in singularly expressive movement, the disturbing conflict between two lovers – or was it meant to portray the travails of an unhappily married couple, surrounded in their anguish by the timeless healing power of Bach's music? An attempt to keep this new Company together after the Festival failed to attract the necessary financial support, and soon afterwards David Poole departed for Cape Town and a new chapter in his professional life.

Two years earlier, in a letter to her family dated the 4th of September 1954, Dulcie Howes (who was on a visit to London) wrote that she had had lunch with David Poole whom she quoted as saying that he wanted to return to South Africa the following year "… to work with my own people". The quotation marks in her letter indicate clearly that these were Poole's precise words. In the event, it was not until after his performances at the 1958 Edinburgh Festival that Poole was able to return to Cape Town 'to work with his own people'.

In an interview published in the magazine *Contact* on the 22nd of February 1958, Poole is quoted as saying that he was determined to found a school of indigenous South African dancing, "… something that will give our dancers a chance to dance as South Africans." Rather curiously, he went on to say: "In Europe our dancers simply cannot do it, as their innate animalistic tendencies have to be toned down to fit in with the existing ballets." In the same interview, David Poole pointed out that, although he was employed by the UCT Ballet School, he hoped to do a lot of work with the Eoan Group "… which I feel has a great future". As we shall see, circumstances – both political and financial – were going to dictate otherwise; but meanwhile Poole certainly enjoyed big successes with two works for the Eoan Group: *Pink Lemonade* and *The Square*. Johaar Mosaval danced the leading roles in both of these hugely popular ballets.

I was not in South Africa at that time, but Marina Grut writes extensively about these ballets in her seminal work: *The History of Ballet in South Africa* (Human and Rousseau, 1981).

"*Pink Lemonade* told the story of Mosaval himself who, from humble beginnings in District Six, became a star in a famous international ballet company. A circus is used as the medium for the story of a group of strolling players who find themselves in competition with a large circus. The son is drawn to the bigger company, leaves his family, and finally appears with them as a star." Poole's second ballet for the Eoan Group was *The Square,* in 1962. It dealt with the struggle between good and evil and took place in a village square. The programme note stated that: "The first carefree games of childhood are threatened by the passion of youth and the violence culminating in the tragedy of a killing. In a dream sequence the gang leader realises his guilt and pleads forgiveness; but the crowd, mistaking his pleadings as a new threat, turn on him and kill him."

Unfortunately, as the Eoan Group's activities dwindled and the racial divide in South Africa became steadily more entrenched, David Poole was destined to find himself directing a 'white' ballet company, constrained by *apartheid* laws as to whom it could employ and where and to whom it was allowed to perform. It was not until the 21st of January 1977 that the first crack appeared in the colour bar at the Nico Malan Opera House: Johaar Mosaval (by now permanently settled in Cape Town) made his first guest appearance with CAPAB Ballet, dancing the title role in *Petrushka*. Both he and Poole had certainly come a long way from their first encounter in a District Six school!

6

Trying For White

As well as being the year in which David Poole returned to Cape Town to work with the Eoan Group, 1959 was also the year in which I was invited to take up a teaching post at my old alma mater, Cape Town University. Coincidentally, it was also in that January that Basil Warner's controversial play, *Try for White,* was staged by The Cockpit Players at Cape Town's Hofmeyer Theatre. It was directed by Leonard Schach with a cast of some of South Africa's most popular actors, including Zoe Randall, Nigel Hawthorne, Heather Lloyd-Jones and Minne Milstein. I don't know whether or not David Poole was able to see this production, but I most certainly did see it; and although that was more than half a century ago, the main themes of the play still resonate with me.

The story, as I recall it, concerned Katrina September, a Cape Coloured woman who was sufficiently pale-skinned to pass for white. She had abandoned her Cape Coloured family and community, changed her name to Catherine Winter and, together with her equally pale-skinned young son, had embarked on a new life in a white suburb. When he reaches adulthood, the boy – who is still unaware of his mother's real roots – falls in love with a white girl from an Afrikaans family. What would happen if his mother's true identity were ever to be unmasked? The moral dilemma posed by the emotional conflict inherent in Basil Warner's play reflected all too convincingly the situation being experienced in many real families. One result of the brutal *apartheid* laws was that, in a number of households, several but not necessarily all members of the same family were able to pass themselves off as white. Was this, perhaps, what had happened to the Poole family?

In 2017, when I was researching this book, I discussed that matter with Jasmine Honoré. Although she was by then already 95 years old, she was still remarkably active and clear-thinking and assured me that she had known David's family very well. She had never met David's father, but had often visited his mother in the family home, in a racially mixed area near Cape Town called Woodstock. At UCT, I had initially known David as one of my tutors; later he became both a colleague and a close friend. When I joined the Ballet School staff David's younger brother, Basil, was one of my most talented students. I recall meeting an older brother, but he was not involved in the dance world. According to Jasmine, David also had two sisters, but I had never come across either of them. Were David's mother and her two daughters perhaps less able to pass as white than the three sons? It has not been possible for me to confirm or deny this nor, indeed, have I been able to ascertain exactly how each member of the Poole family was 'officially classified' by the *apartheid* regime.

There had long been some ambiguity concerning David Poole's true ethnic identity: on the one hand he had clearly been educated in a Coloured school, although this was situated in a racially mixed area. Later, after training and performing with both white and Coloured dancers at UCT, he travelled to the UK to join the SWTB where, according to Peter Wright:

"... we never thought of him as Coloured – to us, he was just another dancer." Then, for the SWTB's South African tour in 1954, Poole was able to be passed off as white, in spite of the fact that the authorities knew full well that he was a Cape Coloured man. Later, on his return to South Africa, in 1959, to work with the Eoan Group, a report published that year in *Die Burger* referred to him quite openly as *"...'n ander Suid-Afrikaanse nie-blanke ballet kunstenaar"* ("another South African non-white ballet artist"). Yet, in 1970, this 'non-white ballet artist' was chosen to succeed Dulcie Howes as Director of the government-funded CAPAB Ballet Company!

Many of the UCT's students were also regularly involved in performances sponsored by The Ballet Club. This was founded by Cecily Robinson when she returned to Cape Town following a promising career in Europe where, as Cécilé Zonova, she had danced with two of the Russian Ballet Companies. The Ballet Club's attitude to racial discrimination seems to have been somewhat more ambivalent than that of Dulcie Howes and the University. The Ballet Club often chose to perform at the Alhambra Theatre, which operated a strict colour bar. A problem arose regarding the participation of the Municipal Orchestra. The Ballet Club's Chairman's annual report for 1945 states that: "The City Council had passed a Minute precluding the participation of the Municipal Orchestra unless non-Europeans were granted admission." (*In South Africa in the late forties and early fifties, the terms non-European or European were commonly used to mean non-White or White South Africans.*)

It is not clear just how the Ballet Club managed to overcome this problem, but it seems that they *were* able to secure the participation of the orchestra *without* African Theatres (who owned the Alhambra) having to rescind their colour bar. Inevitably, this resulted in the Secretary of the Eoan Group writing to the Ballet Club, enquiring what the Club's policy was "… concerning the possibility of non-Europeans applying for admission to the Club." Not surprisingly, at a Ballet Club meeting on the 28th of October, the Minutes stated that: "It was decided that the Secretary should write to the Eoan Group, indicating that it was the opinion of the Committee that there should be no colour bar where dancers are concerned. They should be chosen according to talent only."

Dulcie Howes took a great interest in the activities of the Eoan Group. In its early years, she had herself staged several pieces for them; later, she encouraged most of the senior students on the University's Teacher Training Course, as well as some members of the University Ballet Company, to teach at the Eoan Group and to choreograph ballets for the Group's performances. Prior to their departure to join the Sadler's Wells Theatre Ballet in 1946, those University Ballet Company dancers working with the Eoan Group had included John Cranko and Pamela Chrimes. Ten years later, I was myself teaching and staging ballets for that organisation.

It was also Dulcie Howes who recommended that the Eoan Group should have its own Dance Director. In the early 1950s, Howes decided to groom one of the Group's own dancers, Gwen Michaels, for this post. Gwen – a talented dancer and a charming and intelligent young woman – was duly enrolled for the three-year course at the University. She was greatly assisted by the personal interest and careful guidance given her by Miss Howes, in preparation for this new appointment. As the Eoan Group's Dance Director, Gwen went on to give many years of devoted and enlightened service to her own community.

Sadly, in later years, much of the good work done by Gwen Michaels and others undermined by a power struggle between the Choral and the Dance sections of the Eoan Group; this, eventually, was partly responsible for the decline of the Ballet section. Although David Poole did have two big successes (with *Pink Lemonade* and *The Square*), The Eoan

Group's activities dwindled; the racial divide in South Africa became steadily more entrenched; and David Poole's focus was increasingly directed towards his eventual involvement with the activities of CAPAB.

7

David Poole and CAPAB

In 1963, the South African Government decided to subsidise the arts on a provincial basis. An Administrative Board was established in each of the four provinces to supervise companies presenting performances of ballet, opera, theatre and music. The main sources of funding were to be the then Department of Cultural Affairs and the four Provincial Administrations, with some further assistance from Municipal and Divisional Councils. The problem posed by this plan to establish four separate ballet companies, one in each province, was tackled by the critic, Denis Hatfield, in *The Cape Times* on the 2nd of August, 1965. He wrote that "I feel there is now the comic prospect of professional companies all getting dressed up with nowhere to go for at least half of each year, and not enough first-class dancers to go with them."

Hatfield then proceeded to ask Miss Howes her opinion. Her reply was characteristically sensible, and it would also prove to be prophetic: "The plain fact is that South Africa has neither the theatres nor the theatre public to permit or support four companies continuously on tour with large-scale productions. No centre can support four ballet seasons a year, which seems to be in prospect if each province develops its own professional company. And what about the small places, to many of which the University Ballet had brought ballet for the first time? They lack the necessary facilities for big productions; yet they should – they must – be 'fed' with ballet on a suitable scale."

Howes went on to say that "The ideal arrangement would be for each province to have its own ballet school, with a small company of professionals working alongside the student group (so good for them both) and staging modest indigenous works or extracts from established ballets in the small surrounding towns." (That, of course, was exactly what the UCT Ballet had been doing for many years.) "From these 'reservoirs', groups of dancers could then be chosen to strengthen the main professional company, which would thus have a worthwhile concentration of the best talent available." Hatfield then asked Howes where, in her opinion, the main professional company should be based?

"Does it matter?" Howes replied. "Only one thing is essential: that like the Bolshoi, or the Danish Ballet, or the Royal Ballet, it should be based on a school – a school either existing or founded for that purpose. Think too of the money and effort to be saved by the reduction of managerial and technical staff; and by the cancellation – at one blessed swoop – of the rivalries and jealousies which could so easily strangle South African ballet, standing as it does at the crossroads today! Money is certainly needed, but it must be spent under sensible central control, by people of the theatre, who know what they are buying. Ballet is not big business. It is high art. Let the artists and the practical people of ballet get together – not according to province, but according to the demands of our art. Only in this way will a National Ballet Company flourish here."

Bearing all this in mind, the obvious and sensible thing was for the University Ballet to form the nucleus of what was to become the Cape's new professional ballet company. During the thirty years of its existence, the University Ballet had built up a large, loyal and enthusiastic audience. It also possessed a fine repertoire, good sets and costumes, music scores and, not least, an extremely capable and experienced teaching and technical staff. In spite of this, Dulcie Howes had to fight hard to convince the Government that the University Ballet should be absorbed into the proposed CAPAB organisation, rather than starting a new Cape Province company from scratch, as had been the Government's original intention.

Professor Inskip represented the University of Cape Town on the board of CAPAB and, together with Howes, made the necessary arrangements for this very sensible merger to take place. Initially, the *corps de ballet* was still made up of students who were paid only a basic subsistence allowance, whilst a nucleus of soloists was immediately employed on full-time annual contracts. David Poole was appointed as Ballet Master and Frank Staff as Resident Choreographer. With Howes at the helm, this was indeed a brilliant team. David brought with him the invaluable experience of over a decade with the SWTB, including Peter Wright's endorsement of Poole's skill as a *Repetiteur*; and it is greatly to Dulcie Howes's credit that she chose Frank Staff as CAPAB Ballet's first Resident Choreographer.

Born in South Africa in 1918, of an English father and an Irish mother, Frank Staff studied ballet with Helen Webb and Maude Lloyd before moving to Britain in 1933. He had a distinguished career in Europe, both as dancer and choreographer, before returning to South Africa where he staged a number of his ballets for the University/CAPAB companies in 1963 and 1964. His version of Prokofiev's *Romeo and Juliet,* staged for CAPAB in 1964, was one of the high points in the history of the company. Writing to me soon after the premiere of that ballet, Dulcie Howes waxed lyrical about the ballet's success: "…with David as Romeo, Frank as

Mercutio, John Simons as a *wonderful* Tybalt and a quite superb performance as Juliet by a very slim, emotionally developed Veronica Paeper."

Howes went on to write: "Please don't believe *all* the terrible stories about South Africa and its segregation policy – we still remain an 'open' school." This obviously also related back to the original agreement drawn up between the University, CAPAB and The Dulcie Howes Ballet Trust whereby, within the Cape Town Municipal Area, the Company would be allowed to continue to perform under the name of the University Ballet, and confirming that these performances would be given under the aegis of the Dulcie Howes Ballet Trust. Established originally as long ago as 1942, this Trust had continued to help individual dancers, teachers and choreographers in an educational capacity. This specific agreement between UCT, CAPAB and the DH Trust enabled Howes to use that Trust as a cunning means of circumventing the restrictive clauses concerning multi-racial audiences which governed performances given under the auspices of CAPAB. The provision of this special agreement enabled the company to continue performing to mixed audiences in three venues: the University-owned Little Theatre, the municipality's still un-segregated City Hall, and the Luxurama, at that time still the only commercial multi-racial theatre in the Cape Town area.

In 1970, David Poole was to succeed Dulcie Howes as the Director of the CAPAB Ballet Company. A rumour had been circulating for some time in Cape Town's ballet circles suggesting that David had been offered the Directorship of the Johannesburg Ballet company, and that unless Howes agreed to relinquish her post and arrange for him to be appointed in her place, he would take up the Johannesburg offer. In spite of their unpleasant and often violent disagreements, Howes was well aware of Poole's value to the company and – rather than lose him to Johannesburg – she agreed to his demands. There can be no doubt that, setting aside – as she did – any personal ambition, Dulcie Howes was making a remarkably far-sighted decision in the best interests of her company. Whilst David started to put his stamp on CAPAB Ballet's future development, Howes still remained firmly in charge of the University Ballet School.

For quite some time, the connection between the University Ballet School and CAPAB Ballet remained very close indeed, as most of the dancers engaged by CAPAB were UCT graduates. However, a professional company must engage the best dancers it can find, wherever they have been trained and, in any case, the University could not be regarded primarily as a training establishment for CAPAB dancers. With typical foresight, Howes now saw that the University course needed to be rethought. After retiring as Director of CAPAB Ballet, she began discussions with the University aimed at devising a different type of course. Her plan was to find a formula whereby a more academic framework could be devised through which – without sacrificing the performance element of the UCT course, which she considered so vital – it might be possible to upgrade the Teachers' Certificate course to one of BA status.

Meanwhile, whilst her plans to restructure the course were still in the process of being evaluated by the academic authorities, Howes also set about breathing new life into her student ballet company. In 1972, she was able to accept an invitation for the University Ballet to perform in Lausanne, in Switzerland, as part of an International Festival of Youth Orchestras. The programme Howes chose to present in Lausanne was particularly apt: *Peter and the Wolf* by South Africa's most gifted choreographer, Frank Staff, was a witty character ballet, well within the students' technical capabilities; it gave them the opportunity to display the acting ability which had always been a strong point with South African dancers. The extraordinarily high standard of Spanish dancing taught at UCT certainly guaranteed the success of Marina Keet's *Fiesta Manchega*. The third item chosen by Howes for that Swiss programme was David Poole's *Le Cirque*. It was an inspired choice in that it was able (albeit in coded form) to tackle the vexed question of racial discrimination.

Ostensibly about circus performers ruled by a dictatorial ringmaster, *Le Cirque* was, in fact, intended as a dramatic comment on the repression and social pressures in South African society. It sat well on this multi-racial student company. This was the first time a South African ballet company had performed overseas. For Dulcie Howes, their success and the warmth of their reception represented the culmination of years of pioneering work. One Swiss commentator wrote that: "It would need a miracle to describe in just a few lines the freshness and youth this South African ballet company has brought to Lausanne." At the end of that year, Dulcie Howes was due to retire from the University Ballet School, happy to have revived its fortunes and excited by the prospect of the UCT's planned BA course in ballet. By reading one additional subject, such as Mathematics or English, students were to be able to upgrade the existing Teachers' Certificate to degree status, making it possible for them to be employed as teachers within the State school system.

Alas, David Poole did not see eye-to-eye with Howes in this matter and he succeeded in blocking her plans. Interviewed some ten years later, on the occasion of her 75th birthday, Howes was asked by the journalist Fiona Chisholm whether, looking back over her life and her career, she had any regrets. "If I've had any," she replied, "they would probably have been that I was not able to implement the BA Ballet course at UCT. But I never look back." Why was this so important to Howes? And why did Poole scupper her plans? The fact that neither of them had had the opportunity of acquiring a university education themselves has been suggested as a possible explanation: *she* wanted others to have the education she craved; *he* felt he had reached the top of his profession without needing a university degree, and saw the proposed BA Ballet course as irrelevant. Be that as it may, this was certainly an indication of how Poole planned to operate once he was to be in charge of both the Ballet Company *and* the UCT School.

Over the next few years, Poole put his stamp firmly on the CAPAB Ballet Company. Initially, it certainly flourished under his direction. David appointed Gary Burne as his company's new Resident Choreographer. Burne's *Variations Within Space*, a pure dance work, displayed the increased technical assurance of the whole company. Of Burne's other works, his *Prodigal Son*, danced to an avant-garde score by Subotnik, broke new ground, startling an audience still mainly at home with a more conventional style. The spectacular staging and lighting effects used in this work were made possible by the state-of-the-art equipment of the new Nico Malan Opera House. It had opened on the 19th of May 1972, with Poole's version of Delibes' *Sylvia*.

Later that year, Poole invited me to choreograph two new ballets for CAPAB: *Ritual,* to music by the South African composer, Arnold van Wijk, had designs by another South African, Peter Cazalet – his first work for the company to which he was later to make such a major contribution. My second work was *Venus According*, a light-hearted piece to music by Boyce, with elegant designs by Heather Magoon. That season ended with Marina Keet's much-acclaimed Spanish ballet, *Misa Flamenca*, to a score by Torregrosa, and with a spectacular set by Stephen de Villiers. With Phyllis Spira as CAPAB Ballet's brilliant *prima ballerina*, John Simons as a character artist of rare subtlety, guest artists of the calibre of Johannesburg's Denise Schultze, plus a number of talented young dancers emerging from the University Ballet School, the company was set for an exciting future.

During his long association with CAPAB, David staged several fine productions of the classics, bringing out their full dramatic potential through his unrivalled skill as a stage director. Most of the new ballets he choreographed were rather less distinguished but – on the whole – they served their purpose well by providing suitably varied and challenging roles for his dancers. However, Poole was not in the same league as Staff when it came to new choreography. In an interview on South African television, Owen Murray, a dancer with the company and later Executive Assistant to Poole – as well as a close personal friend – made the point well: "David is not an inventive choreographer. He tells a story exceedingly well. He establishes the characters in a ballet very well indeed; but he's not an original choreographer. Not like Frank Staff, who made you move in a special way."

Poole's Resident Choreographer, Gary Burne, had died at the tragically young age of forty-two; and Frank Staff, who had been Howes' appointee to that post, had also died in 1971. In 1974, Veronica Paeper, who had been married to Frank Staff, was appointed as CAPAB Ballet's new Resident Choreographer. Poole was to remain in charge of the CAPAB Ballet for over two decades – although now that he was also directing the UCT Ballet School and was eventually to become the University of Cape Town's first Professor of Ballet, his official title at CAPAB was changed to that of Artistic Adviser to the Ballet Company. Veronica Paeper remained as Resident Choreographer throughout the remainder of Poole's tenure – and, indeed, well beyond David's retirement and his untimely demise.

In a handsome brochure produced to celebrate CAPAB's 21st birthday, in 1984, Poole described the existing situation as follows: "Even after 21 years of the CAPAB Ballet, it is not easy for people to divorce the Company from the University Ballet School. This is understandable. The Company grew from the UCT Ballet and, even today, through the generosity and far-sightedness of the University of Cape Town, the link has remained and has in many ways been strengthened through the common use of the same training and rehearsal facilities at UCT. Today [1984], the School is a feeder for the Company and the unofficial school of CAPAB Ballet."

Such was the healthy state of affairs when the school Howes had founded was celebrating its fiftieth anniversary. Yet, a little later, although imperceptibly at first, something started to go wrong with the development of ballet in Cape Town. Was this perhaps due in part to the ever-increasing pressures of the cultural boycott that the international community was imposing on South Africa? No doubt some allowances need to be made for the creeping sense of isolation local artists were beginning to suffer due to the growing worldwide opposition to *apartheid*. Yet, before one starts blaming too much on cultural isolation, it is as well to recall that, during the war years, South Africa was effectively cut off from much of the rest of the world. Yet it was precisely during that period that some of the country's finest dancers and most promising choreographers emerged.

One of the main differences between these two separate periods of isolation and their respective effect on the development of an indigenous ballet is that, during the war years, South Africa still looked very much to London for an artistic yardstick. However, during the anti-*apartheid* artistic boycott there was sometimes a tendency for certain South African artists to become increasingly oblivious to artistic developments outside their own country, hiding their heads in the sand, and thereby falling into an understandable, but ultimately self-destructive complacency.

On the surface the company appeared to prosper. Spectacular, expensively-designed productions were staged, making full use of the impressively equipped Nico Malan Opera House and drawing large, enthusiastic audiences. Yet, gradually, a sense of complacency began to permeate local ballet life. In the theatre, skilful staging was all too often used to bolster and camouflage rather banal choreography whilst, within the School, petty rivalries between advocates of competing examination systems blighted relations between some of the dance teachers. It also appears to have been at around the same time that David was to become notorious for his so-called 'short fuse' – his tendency to lose his temper and indulge in shouting matches with more than one conductor of the CAPAB Ballet's orchestra. Adding to all of this the undeniable strain of his having to cope with the perceived ambiguities of his own racial identity, what – in the final analysis – can one assess to have been David Poole's lasting legacy to the art of ballet in his homeland?

8

David Poole's Legacy

David Poole retired from CAPAB in 1991, handing over the direction of the Ballet Company to Veronica Paeper; Elizabeth Triegaardt had already taken over from him earlier at the University Ballet School. Tragically, after a very short illness, David died in hospital that same year, on the 27th of August. In a long speech, soon after Poole's untimely death, Dulcie Howes recalled that: "As a producer he had a truly magical quality. I have vivid memories of David coming into a rehearsal of a ballet which had been carefully taught – the steps of the dancers were neat and accurate and the lines were straight. Within no time at all, David had transformed that ballet into a lively, meaningful and exciting theatrical experience."

Many dancers, teachers and choreographers still continue to credit David for all the help and support he gave them over a number of years. This was, in particular, true of his expert mentoring of young men who had been unable to start serious ballet training until they were already teenagers. A case in point was my former student, Victor Hughes. In an e-mail from Victor, received on Friday the 7th of July 2017, he described to me at some length the importance of David's mentoring, both when he was still a very inexperienced student and, later on, in relation to his work as a Ballet Master. Referring to the latter, Victor wrote: "The lesson learnt was that one has to work from and develop whatever potential those dancers have and not to impose on them impossible or prefabricated ideas."

Unfortunately, some time before David's death, ballet in Cape Town had already started to go into a decline. Was this due to the limitations and the compromises forced on Poole by the political situation or, once he had acquired the directorship of the ballet school *in addition* to that of the company, could David have wanted to prove that he could now wield absolute power? To what extent was his determination to hold onto that power at all costs perhaps due to the psychological problems inherent in the ambiguity of his racial classification? Widely known to be a Cape Coloured man running a government-funded 'white' company must have presented David Poole with an acute moral dilemma.

In spite of the high ideals with which David Poole had originally returned to his homeland "… to work with my own people", he soon found himself having to accept the realities of the changed situation. He knew full well – and told me on more than one occasion – that one way for him to serve his oppressed Coloured fellow artists was by proving to them, *as well as to the government*, that a Coloured man could hold the highest post in the country's ballet world with authority and distinction. He was indeed the perfect role model. Later, when it became clear that, gradually, the ground was being prepared for the release of Nelson Mandela (with all the reforms that were to flow from that), David Poole was able to play an important role as an agent for change, taking a prominent part in the public marches through the streets of Cape Town in defiance of the increasingly compromised *apartheid* government.

Another dilemma that David had to face was the opening in 1971 of the State Theatre in Cape Town named after the Cape

Administrator Nico Malan. The 'Nico', as it became called, was built to house CAPAB performances and, in line with official policy, was for "whites only". This encountered furious protests from artists, critics and members of the public and a boycott of the facility was started. It had widespread support among liberal Capetonians. The theatre was belatedly opened to all in 1975, but the damage had been done and many people, and especially people not classified as "white", continued to observe the boycott until the release of Mandela in 1990.

What of Poole's artistic legacy? He was an incredibly powerful personality and, during his tenure as Director, he had controlled and moulded every aspect of the work of both the Ballet Company and the School. At its best, this dictatorial approach had produced a highly disciplined homogenous ensemble. The flip side was that, in later years, Poole tended more and more to surround himself with "yes-men". As long as he was there to guide them, they served him loyally and efficiently; but, in the end, some (but by no means all) of his successors were to prove unequal to the task. Even in retirement, as well as for several years after his death, David was to continue casting a long shadow over South African ballet.

It seems to have been during the latter years of his directorship of the Company that David was to become somewhat notorious for his so-called 'short fuse' – his tendency to lose his temper, often ending in 'shouting matches' with more than one conductor of the CAPAB orchestra. Discussing this with one of CAPAB Ballet's former stage-managers during my research for this book, I received the following response: "David Poole totally intimidated me. I found his caustic comments thrown out at the dancers from the auditorium often unnecessarily cruel, as was his ability to demolish a dancer in the dressing room with a few words, a look or a gesture. On the plus side, David's performance in *The Rake's Progress* has always remained with me, as has CAPAB Ballet's staging of *The*

Green Table. These were two works which showed that dance can be used to make serious statements, and not only to display the sheer beauty of form and movement in space."

In 1994, the Company – now calling itself the Cape Ballet – presented its first London season. Expectations were very high, thanks to the fine reputation enjoyed by the previous generation of South African dancers and choreographers. British audiences were also prepared to make some allowances for the isolation South African artists had endured during the cultural boycott of their country. Nevertheless, both the repertoire and the standard of dancing shown in London failed to live up to expectations. Sadly, this was true whether judged by international standards or, more importantly, by the very high standard of CAPAB Ballet in the 1970s and early 1980s.

Much was made in the British press of the fact that Veronica Paeper had, reputedly, already choreographed some fifteen full-length ballets for CAPAB. Commenting on this in an interview published in the London magazine *Time Out*, Veronica was quoted as saying: "The public flocks to them. They sell, so one follows the market." That approach struck me as a betrayal of the artistic standards of everyone in South Africa who had worked so hard to produce two generations of world-class dancers, choreographers and teachers. It was an approach which was also symptomatic of some aspects of the malaise still permeating the old South Africa. But what does the new South Africa hold in store for the rather esoteric art of ballet?

The pessimistic view predicts oblivion for what many see as a totally Euro-centric activity and one for which there can be no place in South Africa's changing cultural climate. Personally, I take the more optimistic view – one which considers change healthy, looking positively at the possibilities and the opportunities that lie ahead. Dulcie Howes's legacy – and that of her many associates – lives on in the huge number of talented and experienced dancers, teachers, choreographers and technicians she trained and inspired, as well as in the vast, enthusiastic audiences she helped create throughout Southern Africa. I have no doubt that many South Africans will be able to meet the challenges offered by the changing culture now emerging in their country.

It is impossible to predict the ways in which this new culture will evolve, and it will probably take several generations for a truly multi-racial society to develop and for genuinely multi-cultural art forms to crystallise. It seems to me that, once again, the University of Cape Town could play an important part in these developments. Just as the genesis of a European-style South African ballet company can be traced back to the University Ballet School, so too could an imaginatively run University Dance Department help to sow the seeds of future South African dance. Unfortunately, in recent years, the UCT Dance School has been run with too narrow a concept of what ballet is or could become. That was perhaps to some extent understandable in the circumstances in which the school had to operate once the CAPAB Ballet Company had come to dominate the scene. But these are new times in South Africa and the future of dance must now follow different paths, re-inventing itself in ways we cannot foresee, but which I, for one, await with high hopes. And that is a sentiment which I am quite certain that both Dulcie Howes *and* David Poole would have shared.

9

The International Influence of UCT
Graduates and CAPAB Dancers

Nowadays, Dance Departments are a feature of universities and colleges in many countries; but the University of Cape Town seems to have been one of the first in the field. Hundreds of ballet teachers working either in South Africa or abroad were trained at UCT. However, the genesis of this particular Dance Department was so unusual that it needs to be understood before examining the changing nature of the Teacher-Training Course it was to offer.

Cape Town University already had a lively Speech and Drama Department and a flourishing Faculty of Music when the Dean of that Faculty, Professor W. H. Bell, first invited Dulcie Howes to start what was later to develop into the University Ballet School. Howes had recently returned to her native South Africa following a lengthy study period in Europe, culminating in an engagement to dance with the Anna Pavlova Ballet Company; she had then opened a private dancing school in the Cape Town suburb of Rondebosch. In 1932, Professor Bell now invited Dulcie Howes to transfer her dancing school to a room in the university's College of Music; but it would take a little more persuasion from Professor Bell for Howes to give up her precious independence and agree to her school becoming an official department of the University's Faculty of Music. The year was 1934.

In 1953, when I enrolled as a full-time student at the University Ballet School, the core curriculum was still very much what it had been when that course was first established: essentially practical, and strongly geared to performing in the theatre, but with a sound theoretical component too. Later on, there were to be various changes, in both content and emphasis. I will return to these but, first of all, I want to look more closely at the unique nature of the course as it was originally conceived (and as it still operated in the early 1960s), stressing how it differed from the types of courses which are now the norm in the dance departments of most universities and colleges.

Dulcie Howes believed passionately that teachers of dance cannot be trained exclusively in the classroom. She insisted that no one could become a really good dance teacher unless he or she had had some stage experience, no matter at how humble a level. Therefore, during the first thirty years of its existence – and until the emergence of CAPAB – Cape Town University's dance department encompassed a Ballet Company *as well as* a Teacher-Training School.

In every aspect of the university's Teacher-Training course the emphasis was on the integration of the theoretical aspects of study into their practical execution. Although there were regular lectures to attend, essays to write and projects to prepare, followed up by compulsory written examinations, the purely academic content of the Teachers' Certificate course was limited. Under Dulcie Howes, learning to teach was very much a "hands on" affair. There was a large and thriving Junior School connected to the University Ballet. It was here, on several afternoons a week, that each student was assigned to assist a member of staff in the practicalities of teaching ballet to children. This was very much an apprentice system and I now realise just how sensible and successful that approach to teacher-training had been.

The more senior students were sent out to teach on a regular basis at various community centres and schools. This often led to opportunities to choreograph and to assist in the staging of school shows. Our mornings were taken up with our own dancing classes and with lectures; the afternoons were devoted to teaching practice and private study. Many evenings and weekends were spent rehearsing for the University Ballet Company's performances. Full-time really meant just that when one worked with Dulcie Howes.

Those performances took place mainly during the university's vacation periods. The UCT Ballet Company consisted entirely of students, with some members of the teaching staff dancing the leading roles. During my time as a student (1953 – 1956) these included three UCT graduates who had gone on to dance professionally in Europe, prior to returning to teach us at UCT. They were Pamela Chrimes, who had been a soloist with the SWTB, Jasmine Honoré, who had danced with London's Ballet Rambert, and Mary Silberbauer, who had been with Massine's Ballet du Châtelet de Paris. During this period David Poole (SWTB) and Petrus Bosman (London Festival ballet) also returned to Cape Town as guest artists. It was from these five people that we students learned so much about stagecraft.

There was no question of anyone being paid for performances and neither the University nor the State gave the Ballet Company financial support. The Faculty of Fine Art was persuaded to help with the design of costumes and the painting of stage scenery, and members of the Faculty of Music were cajoled into forming a small touring orchestra. For performances in towns within a reasonable driving distance from Cape Town, friends and parents were persuaded not only to provide transport, but also to act as stage hands, dressers and electricians. For tours further afield, various Arts Associations, educational authorities and charitable institutions would invite the company to visit their town or city. They saw this partly as a chance to introduce their community to what, in South Africa, was still a new form of entertainment; but they also regarded these performances as a means of fund-raising. The host organisation would meet the cost of travel expenses and publicity, as well as the hire of the theatre and the front-of-house staff.

These sponsors were also given the unenviable task of arranging accommodation with private families for all the dancers, musicians and other personnel. Dulcie Howes actually saw this system of billeting the dancers with local families as a valuable way of building audiences. She later told me that: "The hosts, who had probably never seen ballet and didn't really want to, were dragged to performances by their wives, or else because they felt they owed it to their house guests. It was hard work educating the public as well as the dancers."

Gradually, thanks to the devoted work of so many unpaid dancers, musicians and technicians, the University Ballet slowly started to make enough to actually pay for some guest artists. During my third year as a student, two particularly distinguished guest artists performed with us: Nadia Nerina and Alexis Rassine, who were both stars from the Sadler's Wells Company at Covent Garden. Interestingly, they had trained in South Africa *prior* to the founding of the UCT Ballet. Nerina was a pupil of Eileen Keegan in Durban; Rassine was from Cape Town, a pupil of Helen Webb and Maude Lloyd. How lucky we were to be able to perform alongside artists of their calibre!

From the mid-sixties, the essential nature of the three-year course at the UCT Ballet School was destined to change. This was when the possibility of state funding for the arts was first mooted. The sensible thing was now going to be for the University Ballet to form the nucleus of the new CAPAB Ballet Company. Within two years the metamorphosis was complete and a fully professional ballet company had come into being. Although most of the dancers engaged by CAPAB had been UCT graduates, the University could not be regarded primarily as a training establishment for CAPAB dancers: a professional company must engage the best dancers it can find, wherever they have been trained.

Various adjustments were made to the UCT course. These were aimed at streaming the students into either potential teachers or potential professional dancers. None of these experiments proved to be really satisfactory and they led to discontent among the students. A feeling had begun to develop that those students who were being channelled towards teaching rather than performing were considered "second class citizens" – a ridiculous situation to have on a University-based course. Although a (much reduced) performing element was still a part of the teacher-training stream, with the now-dominant presence of the CAPAB Ballet Company, the heart had gone out of what remained of the University Ballet Company.

With typical foresight, Howes now saw that the University course needed to be totally re-thought. In 1969, after retiring as Director of the CAPAB Ballet Company, she entered into discussions with the University aimed at devising a different type of course. Her plan was to find a formula whereby a more academic framework could be devised (without sacrificing the performance element which she considered so vital) so that the University could be persuaded to upgrade the Teachers' Certificate Course to BA Status. As we have already seen, this would later lead to a serious disagreement with David Poole.

My own instinct is against undue academic influence. I have seen too many new-fangled dance degree courses mushrooming in Britain – BAs, MAs and even Doctorates awarded to people with insufficient *practical* understanding of their subject. Personally, I gained a great deal from the old, original UCT Ballet Certificate course. Yet one must recognise that it existed at a particular time, in specific and unusual circumstances. It was also run by some very special people. Different times and changed circumstances call for new solutions.

A remarkable number of the dancers trained at UCT went on to dance professionally either overseas or else in South Africa, with the CAPAB Ballet or the other new, state-funded Ballet Companies. Some found themselves in demand as Ballet or Spanish Dance teachers, either at home or abroad, whilst others enjoyed successful careers performing with a variety of dance companies in Europe or the USA. Several of these were given the opportunity to continue developing their choreographic talents with those companies. One or two others either founded their own companies or were invited to stage works for existing ones.

The following is an overview of a few of those dancers, and/or teachers, who were able to influence the development of dance in Europe, in the USA, or in Turkey:

Petrus Bosman: Petrus was born in 1928 in Kuilsrivier, in the Western Cape. As a teenager he enrolled in ballet classes at UCT, where he was trained by Dulcie Howes and Cecily Robinson. He graduated from UCT in 1949 and then travelled to Europe where he continued his studies with Anna Northcote prior to joining the London Festival Ballet Company. He soon became a Soloist and later a Principal dancer with that company. Some of his most successful performances were in the famous Fokine ballet *Petrushka*, in which he danced both the title role and that of the Moor, as well as playing the character role of the magician who presents the puppet show which tells the story of Petrushka's unrequited love for the Ballerina. In 1955, on a visit to Cape Town, Bosman also staged *Petrushka* for the UCT Ballet Company.

In 1959, Petrus Bosman joined The Royal Ballet as a Soloist, advancing rapidly through the ranks to the status of Principal, performing the leading male roles in *Giselle* and *The Sleeping Beauty*, as well as character roles in *The Firebird* and *The Lady and the Fool*. During his eighteen years in London, Bosman also staged a series of hugely successful Charity Galas, featuring such stars as Margot Fonteyn, Merle Park, Antoinette Sibley, Anthony Dowell, Rudolf Nureyev and Johaar Mosaval.

When Petrus retired from dancing, Rosella Hightower invited him to teach at her school in Cannes. He then went on to direct the Jeune Ballet de France, where he was also able to make full use of the teaching experience he had acquired at UCT. In 1977 Bosman moved to the USA, where he first worked with the Maryland Ballet, before becoming director of public relations with the Cultural Arts Program in Baltimore, where he was tasked with engaging leading dancers, singers and musicians to perform at the Lyric Theatre. He was later appointed Director of the Virginia School of the Arts, a post he held for seventeen years before finally retiring in 2006.

Marina Grut (née Keet): Marina was born in 1934, in Calvinia, a small town in the barren but beautiful Karoo. In her autobiography *My Dancing Life – Spanish and Ballet Across Three Continents* (The Book Guild, 2017) Marina Grut writes nostalgically about her early childhood in Calvinia; but it was not until her parents settled in Stellensosch, some 50 kilometres from Cape Town, that the young Marina was to experience the first inklings of what was going to become an amazingly rich and diverse "Dancing Life".

Marina was ten years old when she joined the little dancing school situated just across the road from the new family home in Stellenbosch. She took to dancing like a duck to water and, in her own words, has said that: "My fate was sealed". A few years later, her ambition to study at UCT was going to be encouraged by Cecily Robinson; but by then her teacher in Stellenbosch, Amelia Conn – who was leaving to get married – had persuaded Marina to take over her dancing school. Combining teaching in Stellenbosch with the three-year Ballet Certificate course at UCT was going to be enormously demanding; but with the moral support and encouragement of Dulcie Howes, Marina was able to embark on the gruelling but stimulating experience which she describes in great detail in Chapter 2 of her autobiography.

Marina and I were fellow students at UCT. She had enrolled on the course one year before me, but we shared many interests and soon became firm friends. In particular, we were both very keen to try our hand at choreography. Our activities on that front are enthusiastically recounted on pages 28 to 31 of Marina's autobiography. That fascination with choreography was to last throughout our lives as was, indeed, the close friendship between our respective families. An important element in Marina's future choreography was to be her passionate interest in all aspects of Spanish dance.

Our Spanish dance tutor at UCT, Jasmine Honoré, had studied in London with the legendary Elsa Brunelleschi. Marina then also went on to study with Brunelleschi and was encouraged by her to embark on a series of visits to Spain to study with several of Spain's most knowledgeable dancers and teachers. As well as continuing her exploration of the subtle differences between various styles of Flamenco, she developed a particular interest in the rich variety of Spain's regional dances and also in the Escuela Bolera, the exhilarating traditional classical dances of Spain. Later, Marina undertook a special, in-depth study of the mysterious dances of the Basques.

Following the founding of the Spanish Dance Society (SPD)

by a group of Spanish dance teachers in South Africa in 1956, Marina Grut's extensive knowledge of Spanish dance and her deep understanding of Spanish culture were soon to become instrumental in the creation of a Spanish dance syllabus. This syllabus was designed to explain and facilitate the teaching of Spanish dancing in a logical and carefully calibrated way. As the work of the South African SPD began gaining interest abroad, it turned into the International Spanish Dance Society, whose syllabus is now taught and examined in Britain, Italy, Greece, Malta, America, Australia, Thailand, Canada and Mexico, as well as in Spain itself. A truly astonishing achievement by a dedicated team of dancers and teachers, inspired by Marina, but who had all worked together on a purely voluntary basis for many a long hour to refine and expand their teaching methods.

After their marriage in 1959, Marina and Mikael Grut settled down to a new life in Sweden. Marina spent their first few months there setting up house and learning Swedish. However, she soon yearned to be somehow involved in the theatre again. Dulcie Howes had given her a letter of introduction to Mary Skeaping, the artistic director of Stockholm's ballet company. Unfortunately, at that time, it was impossible for the theatre to employ Marina and Skeaping suggested that she might instead start researching Swedish dance history. She began that research in the Royal Library with the help of Mikael Grut's librarian aunt Margit. Little could Marina have imagined that, many decades later, her research would result in the publication of her monumental *Royal Swedish Ballet History 1592 to 1962*.

In 1961, Marina and Mikael returned to South Africa – Mikael to lecture in Stellenbosch and Marina to take over the teaching of Spanish dancing at UCT. The next few years were destined to be both busy and challenging for ballet in South Africa in general, and for Marina Grut in particular. Among many other offers of work, she was asked to arrange the dances in numerous operas and plays. Yet the most exciting event in the development of ballet in South Africa was still to come in 1964: the long-awaited establishment of state-funded professional companies like the CAPAB Ballet. For them Marina was to choreograph several new works, including *The Three-Cornered Hat*, with Phyllis Spira and Gary Burne starring in the leading roles. But soon the Gruts would be on the move again – this time to Italy.

In 1977 Mikael had been offered a good post in Rome, with the Food and Agriculture Organisation of the United Nations (FAO). Marina felt that, what with setting up house again and coping with all the related responsibilities, it would be sensible for her to stop teaching. However, following the repeated efforts of several local teachers wanting to get her to teach them the Spanish Dance Society's syllabus, she did eventually relent. This heralded the start of what was to become the still-flourishing Italian branch of the SPD.

The Gruts were finding life in Rome stressful on a number of levels. They had thought that the move to Italy was intended to be permanent; but after four hard years they were pleasantly surprised when Mikael was appointed forestry specialist at the World Bank in Washington DC. The move to the USA in 1981 would turn out to be particularly exciting for the opportunities it held in store for Marina. Both of the Gruts' older children had remained in Europe to continue their studies, so once the younger son, Nicolai, aged eleven, was settled in a good school, Marina set about surveying the Washington dance scene.

She had an introduction to Mary Day of the Washington Ballet who was very welcoming, but who was, at that time, unable to help her. They would later become good friends and colleagues. With Mary Day unable to employ her, Marina approached the Department of Theatre and Dance at George Washington University. She was first asked to teach a masterclass there, to demonstrate her credentials. The difficult conditions in which that class took place are recorded in detail on pages

180 and 181 of Marina's autobiography. Nevertheless, Marina was almost immediately appointed to the post of Professional Lecturer at George Washington University.

All the presentations of Spanish dance in the Washington area were of flamenco; but Marina was determined to show audiences the vast range of styles and techniques which make Spanish regional dances some of the richest in the world. With her typical courage and enthusiasm, but without any financial backing, she bravely set about starting the Spanish Dance Theatre Company. A number of professional dancers were eager to learn the wonderful material Marina had acquired during her many visits to Spain and were willing to dance for the Company without payment. Many people commented on the way they all collaborated with a common purpose: to perform these wonderful dances to the highest possible standard.

During the next few years, Marina was to receive many plaudits for her propagation of the syllabus of the Spanish Dance Society internationally, as well as for the performances of her Spanish Dance Theatre Company in both Washington and New York. In 1989, the importance of Marina's work was recognised when she received a letter informing her that King Juan Carlos of Spain had honoured her with the title of Dame of the Order of Queen Isabel Of Spain, *Lazo de Dama de la Orden de Isabel la Catolica*. This was the highest decoration bestowed on a foreign national by the government of the time. The Spanish Ambassador to the United States, Julian Santamaria, presented Marina with the accompanying medal at a ceremony in Washington DC in February 1989.

At the World Bank, where Marina's husband Mikael worked, all employees were required to retire at the age of sixty-two. Although Marina had been very happy in Washington, in October 1993 the Gruts decided, for family reasons, to settle in London. Marina continued to work closely with the SPD as their President; she also became involved in the often-controversial deliberations of the British Council for Dance Education and Training. In 2007, as part of a performance called *Beyond Flamenco*, Marina was invited to present a special lecture-demonstration; this took the form of a celebration of the rich variety of Spanish dance styles, something which Marina had always championed. Although she continued to be active on many fronts, much of Marina's time was now taken up with writing her autobiography.

TURKISH BALLET and the remarkable UCT connection: In 1947, with Western classical music and Opera, as well as some examples of Western Theatre, already influencing the culture of the Turkish Democratic Republic, the government decided to introduce classical ballet to the growing number of theatre audiences. The Turks decided therefore to invite Ninette de Valois (founder of London's Sadler's Wells Ballet – later renamed The Royal Ballet) to look into the possibility of establishing a ballet school in Turkey, a country with no tradition and very little understanding of classical ballet. Geographically, it would have been logical for the Turks to have called on their Russian neighbours to do this, rather than on the British – but the Cold War had started and both the Turkish and the British governments were anxious to keep the Russians and any possible spread of communist ideas out of Turkey.

Russia had a much older and more distinguished ballet tradition than Britain; but the Russians had already embarked on the process of sending some of their ballet teachers to neighbouring countries to champion the spread of communist sympathies. The British Foreign Office was therefore very supportive of Ninette de Valois' acceptance of the Turkish government's invitation. Later, she would jokingly speak of having played the role of a sort of Mata Hari figure in the development of ballet in Turkey. During the following decade,

81

de Valois arranged for a succession of British teachers and choreographers to take turns in running the new Turkish State Ballet School. They were tasked with training the first group of future Turkish ballet students up to the level where they could form the nucleus of the first Turkish State Ballet Company.

By the mid-1960s, the new Turkish State Ballet Company was well established and had started performing 19th century classics like *Coppélia* and *Giselle,* as well as ballets such as Frederick Ashton's *Les Patineurs* and Ninette de Valois' *The Rake's Progress.* Having retired as Director of The Royal Ballet in 1963, Dame Ninette de Valois was now able to spend more time nurturing the Turkish State Ballet Company by paying frequent visits to Ankara to supervise their progress. Feeling that the Turkish dancers were now strong enough for her to stage *Swan Lake* for them, she decided she would need a new, young Ballet Master to assist her in coaching the dancers and supervising the *Swan Lake* rehearsals. Interestingly, the young man she appointed as her new Ballet Master was the South African UCT graduate, **Dudley Tomlinson**.

Born in South Africa's Kruger National Park where his father was a game ranger, Dudley was seven when his parents moved to Somerset East where he first started ballet lessons. When his father died, Dudley and his mother moved to Cape Town where he was auditioned by Dulcie Howes who encouraged him to register for the UCT Teacher-Training Course. With the help of fine teachers like David Poole and Pamela Chrimes, Dudley was soon dancing solo roles with the UCT Ballet Company and touring with them throughout Southern Africa. Following his graduation from UCT, Dudley arrived in London in 1960 to complete his training at the Royal Ballet School. Before long he had joined the Royal Ballet Company and was dancing in the classical repertoire as well as in ballets by Ashton and MacMillan. Sadly, during his second year in the Royal Ballet, Dudley suffered a serious injury and was advised to stop dancing for quite some time. It was during this period that de Valois had watched him teach a company class. Impressed by his teaching ability and aware of his UCT background, she kept an eye on him and eventually offered him the post of Ballet Master in Turkey.

At that time, I was a soloist and a guest choreographer with the Scapino Ballet in Amsterdam, but my wife Heather and I often met up with Dudley during our summer holidays in London. I was intrigued by his stories about working in Turkey with de Valois. I had been thinking of moving back to London and as I actually had a letter of introduction to Ninette de Valois from Dulcie Howes, I questioned Dudley closely about her, trying to find out a little more about this famous but formidable lady. I was hoping that she might be able to offer me some work in the UK and I decided to write to her. She asked me to come and see her and we had a long chat in her garden in Barnes. She questioned me about the choreography I had been doing in Holland and eventually said, "I don't have anything to offer you here, but would you like to come to Turkey?"

In those days Turkey still seemed to me to be a somewhat dauntingly remote and exotic country. I discussed de Valois' proposal with my wife, Heather; she has always been more adventurous than I am and soon persuaded me to accept the post of Resident Choreographer to the Turkish State Opera and Ballet Companies, situated in the Capital, Ankara. This was going to be an enormous privilege for a young choreographer. I was just thirty years old, and not only was I going to have a full ballet company at my disposal, but I would be working alongside one of the most experienced and prestigious ladies in the ballet world.

I had experienced life during some of the early pioneering years of South African ballet. When I arrived in Ankara in 1965 Turkish ballet was also still emerging from *its* pioneering days; and although the situation I found in Ankara was in many ways different to that which I had left behind a decade earlier in Cape Town, it was also not entirely dissimilar. The Ballet Company I was to work with now was very much like the CAPAB Ballet for which, at David Poole's invitation, I had created two one-act ballets: *Ritual* and *Venus According*. In Ankara, not only was I going to have to arrange dances for various opera productions as well as creating a one-act work on a Turkish theme, to a score by a Turkish composer, but Dame Ninette also encouraged me to choreograph the first 3-act ballet to be created for the Turkish State Company: *Sylvia* – my own interpretation of Delibes' famous score. The premiere took place on the 25th of January 1967, in celebration of the 20th anniversary of de Valois' founding of the Turkish State Ballet School. The following season I created my second 3-act ballet, *The Prince of the Pagodas*, to a score by Benjamin Britten.

When I first arrived in Ankara, I was one of only two choreographers to create new works for the Company's repertoire – there were as yet no indigenous choreographers. Dame Ninette's next mission was going to be to rectify that situation. With her instinctive flair for 'spotting' latent talent, she set about mentoring young Oytun Turfanda, a highly intelligent recent graduate from the State Conservatoire. He responded splendidly, avidly absorbing as much as possible from watching me choreographing new material, and he soon developed into a most interesting choreographer. This sparked off a new fascination with choreography among several other members of the Company. Drawing on the experience Marina Keet and I had had in our student choreographic workshops at UCT, I was able to devise practical ways of helping some of these new, aspiring choreographers.

Dame Ninette had been intent on persuading the Turks to explore their rich tradition of folk dance as the basis from which to develop a truly indigenous style of choreography. Although she *was* able to encourage a few Turkish musicians to compose ballet scores, it would still take some time for a choreographer like Turfanda to fulfil all of his mentor's expectations regarding the realisation of a truly Turkish ballet style. Prior to that, Turkish audiences were really more interested in looking to the West, and the Director of the State Opera Company was busily staging German or Italian operas with cumbersome designs, totally unsuitable for ballet. Meanwhile, by encouraging the young Osman Şengezer to design excellent sets and costumes for my staging of *Sylvia*, she was able to set him on the path to becoming Turkey's most successful designer for both ballet *and* opera.

In 1968 the South African influence on Turkish ballet was further increased when we invited Pamela Chrimes to stage two of John Cranko's ballets in Ankara: *Pineapple Poll* and *Beauty and the Beast*. That same year another former Cape Town dancer, Alfred Rodrigues, created the ballet *Three Sisters* for us, to a score by Ginastera. Rodrigues had already acquired a fine reputation in England with his ballet *Blood Wedding*, based on Garcia Lorca's *Bodas de sangre*. The following year he re-staged it in Ankara with huge success. The theme of this work was particularly suited to the dramatic qualities of the Turkish dancers and it was to mark the start of Rodrigues' decade-long association with Turkish ballet. When a second State Ballet Company was founded in Istanbul Rodrigues created many new ballets for them, including his own spectacularly successful version of Prokofiev's *Romeo and Juliet*.

During the first few months of my time in Ankara, Dudley's injury had started to heal sufficiently for him to be able to dance again. This was very convenient, because although the Turkish male dancers were very talented, they could be somewhat unreliable. With *Swan Lake* being performed at least once a week, Dudley was able to fill in for any absent dancer in the demanding first act *pas de trois*. At the end of my 2nd year, Dudley decided to return to the UK to dance with the Royal Ballet. At the end of my 3rd year I too was beginning to consider returning to London, hoping that after working closely for three years with Dame Ninette, she might consider employing me in some capacity in England. In fact, she told me that if I would agree to stay on in Ankara for one more season, she would arrange for me to join the teaching staff at White Lodge, the Royal Ballet's Lower School in London's Richmond Park.

I was to remain on the teaching staff of the Royal Ballet School for the following seventeen years. During that time, I held the posts of Senior Teacher for Boys at White Lodge and Director of Choreographic Studies at the Royal Ballet's Upper School. My subsequent career as a teacher, choreographer and writer is recorded in my autobiography *Congo to Covent Garden* (Blurb Books, London, 2015). In addition to Petrus Bosman, Marina Grut, Dudley Tomlinson and me, many other UCT graduates were employed in various companies in Europe or the USA. Before considering some of *their* achievements, I would like to underline the important link which existed between David Poole and Ninette de Valois by referring my readers to the correspondence between Dulcie Howes and de Valois which has already been alluded to in Chapter Two.

Referring to her offer to award David Poole a scholarship to continue his studies at the Royal Ballet School, de Valois had written to Miss Howes saying "…now that we are developing, it is my intention to draw our male dancers from Australia, South Africa and Canada." The year was 1946 and British ballet was still recovering from the losses it had suffered during World War II. Ninette de Valois needed to find ways to rebuild her ballet company. One important way in which this could be done was by drawing on the talent available in South Africa and other Commonwealth countries. In 1946, when Ninette de Valois was writing to Dulcie Howes concerning David Poole's future, the Sadler's Wells Theatre Ballet was already employing another UCT graduate, John Cranko, who was rapidly developing into a very gifted young choreographer. Johaar Mosaval was to join the SWTB a year or two after Cranko and Poole, whilst Pamela Chrimes had already been dancing with them since late 1945 and was soon to be joined by Patricia Miller and several other South African dancers.

Ninette de Valois had, of course, pioneered the development of ballet in England. Following her retirement from The Royal Ballet, she again eagerly threw herself into the pioneering task of building a ballet company in Turkey. In both instances, de Valois undoubtedly drew upon much of what she had learned from her time as a soloist with Diaghilev's Ballet Russe. Anyone who was later lucky enough to have the opportunity to work with this remarkable woman will, in one way or another, have become the beneficiary of her exposure to the Ballet Russe and the extraordinary array of ground-breaking artists, choreographers and composers, and the many gifted dancers employed by Serge Diaghilev. This certainly applied to Petrus Bosman, Marina Grut, Dudley Tomlinson and me, as it will also have affected, in various ways, the following small selection of other UCT graduates who have gone on to work professionally all over the world in a number of different fields.

Johaar Mosaval: Johaar was born on the 8th of January 1928 in Cape Town. His early years in South Africa have already been covered in Chapter Two, and Sir Peter Wright's personal recollections of Mosaval and his family were mentioned in Chapter Four. Following Johaar's brilliant career in Europe, first as a Soloist and then as a Principal Dancer with both the Sadler's Wells Theatre Ballet and London's Royal Ballet at Covent Garden, Johaar received the Queen Elizabeth Silver Jubilee Medal in 1977 for his services to ballet in the United Kingdom. Mosaval then returned to Cape Town where he opened a private ballet school, teaching pupils of all races. The school was eventually shut down by the authorities because

Mosaval was ignoring the relevant *apartheid* legislation regarding separate educational facilities for specific racial groups. Johaar was also the first mixed-race dancer to perform on the stage of the Nico Malan Opera House, in David Poole's staging of *Petrushka* for the CAPAB Ballet. Following the release of Mandela and the new South African government's eradication of all *apartheid* legislation, Mosaval was awarded the Western Cape Arts Culture and Heritage Medal for his contribution to the performing arts in South Africa, and in 2005 he was also awarded the Cape Tercentenary Foundation's Molteno Gold Medal.

Peter Cazalet: Peter was born in 1934 in Northern Rhodesia and had started studying architecture at Cape Town University prior to enrolling at the Ballet School. Following his graduation, he danced in the UK with London's Festival Ballet before becoming a Principal with Western Theatre Ballet (later the Scottish Ballet) where he remained for 18 years. During that time, he also designed several of their productions. Peter returned to South Africa in 1972 where he was to head the CAPAB Design Department with great distinction for many years.

Harold King: After graduating from UCT, Harold joined the CAPAB Ballet Company as a soloist. When he moved to Britain he danced with the Scottish Ballet before deciding to found his own very successful ballet company, the London City Ballet, in 1978. Diana, Princess of Wales, took a particular interest in King's work and was the Company's Patron from 1983 until 1996 when, sadly, for financial reasons, London City Ballet had to close. In 1998 Harold King was appointed Artistic Director of Spain's Ballet de Zaragoza. For health reasons, Harold later returned to South Africa for a while. He still continues to take an active interest in ballet both in Europe and in South Africa

THE INTERNATIONAL INFLUENCE

where, in 2005, he became involved with DFA, choreographing a dance piece for their Youth Company.

Terence Etheridge: Terence moved to Britain soon after completing his UCT training and was initially employed as a soloist with the London Festival Ballet. In a long and very successful and varied career, Terence has worked as a dancer and choreographer in ballet, opera and musical theatre, and as a ballet teacher at the Rambert School and at the Urdang Academy. He has also been employed as Ballet Master for the Northern Ballet Theatre and as Artistic Director of the Hong Kong Ballet Company. Terence Etheridge now works as the main choreographer with the Duchy Ballet Company in Cornwall, where the Ballet Mistress, Sianne Strasburg, was also another UCT graduate.

Diane van Schoor: Diane danced with great success as a soloist with the CAPAB Ballet before being promoted to performing principal roles with the Company prior to moving to England. In London, as well as working as a guest teacher with The Royal Ballet Company, Diane was also appointed to the Artistic Staff of both the Lower and the Upper sections of the Royal Ballet School. Subsequently, Diane became the Ballet Principal at White Lodge, the Royal Ballet Lower School in Richmond Park, a post she fulfilled with great distinction for some ten years. Diane is currently very much in demand as a guest teacher all over the world, as well as working as a Consultant to several vocational training programmes. She is also an International Examiner for the Cecchetti Society. Diane was delighted when I told her that I was writing this book. She told me that she had loved working with David Poole: "I learnt so much from him – unknowingly – but which was so valuable when I opened my own school, especially on the production side."

It is impossible to list all the UCT graduates who worked overseas, but here are three examples:

Susan Collins and her Spanish husband José toured a number of countries with great success in a most original act which included various acrobatics and sometimes a little pointe work for Susan. **Karen Langerman** danced professionally in Germany from 1955 to 1957 with the Hanover Ballet under the direction of Yvonne Georgi, whilst **Len Martin** was a soloist with the Scapino Ballet in Amsterdam, whose director, Hans Snoek, later employed me as a soloist and choreographer.

Dulcie Howes, Founder of UCT Ballet School and Director of CAPAB
Ballet. *Photo Rose Jennings*

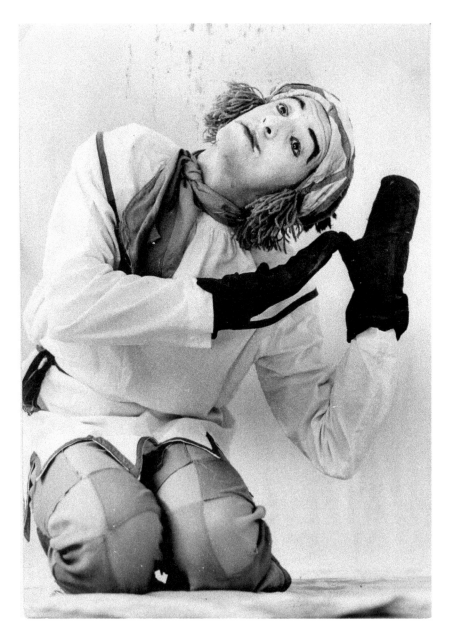

Richard Glasstone in Petrus Bosman's staging of *Petrushka* for the UCT Ballet.
Photo UCT

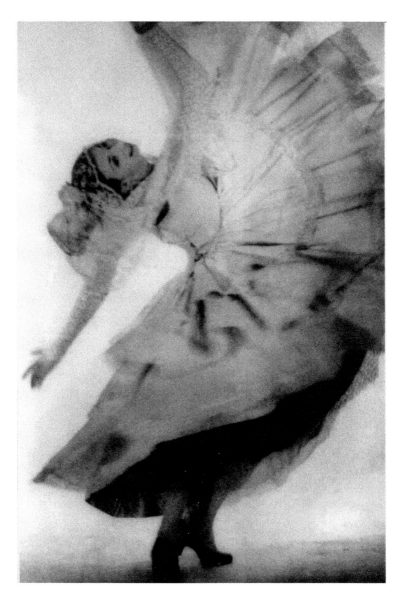

Marina Keet (Mrs M Grut) performing a Spanish dance at the age of 21.
Photo Melvin Duncan

Dame Ninette de Valois with Dudley Tomlinson.
Photo courtesy of Dance for All

Dame Ninette at a stage call with Dudley Tomlinson and designer Osman
Şengezer. *Photo DFA*

Johaar Mosaval in David Poole's 1977 staging of Petrushka.
Photo Keith Mackintosh

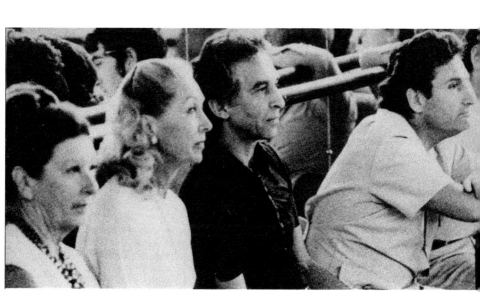

Cecily Robison with CAPAB Ballet Director David Poole, and conductor
David Tidbold. *Photo Odin*

Past students on Ballet School steps. Centre: Poole, John Simons & Johaar
Mosaval. *Photo Argus*

10

Dance for All

In 1990, on his retirement as Artistic Director of CAPAB Ballet, David Poole was eager to devote much more of his time and energy to continuing the work he had already started doing with a small group of male students in the township of Nyanga. Unfortunately, due to the increasing amount of unrest in Nyanga and several other townships, it became temporarily impossible for that type of Outreach work to continue. Sadly, David Poole died the following year. Soon after that, Philip Boyd, a leading dancer with CAPAB Ballet and a great admirer of David's, decided that it was time for CAPAB Ballet to widen its vision by becoming involved in the dance training of young children in a number of disadvantaged communities.

Philip Boyd discussed this idea with Veronica Paeper, who had succeeded David Poole as CAPAB Ballet's Artistic Director. Boyd and Paeper both agreed that in order to promote the further development of classical ballet among all races in South Africa, it was becoming increasingly desirable for them to try to fulfil David Poole's ultimately thwarted vision of establishing a viable educational Outreach Programme in the townships on the outskirts of Cape Town. Harsh living conditions were the norm in those townships or, as they were sometimes euphemistically called, 'informal settlements'. The traditional white face of ballet in South Africa was changing. There were certainly a number of 'coloured' dancers but 'black' dancers were rare. The best way to address that was to start teaching ballet to black children. This resulted in the creation of Ballet for All.

Philip wanted to make ballet as popular as sport and to take it out to disadvantaged communities, so that it would cease to be seen as something essentially elitist. The fact that Philip was a male ballet teacher did, of course, help to attract more boys to his classes. He hoped that eventually ballet might be able to become a source of career opportunities for some of these young men. Gradually, as Ballet for All started to employ teachers working in various dance styles other than classical ballet, it became logical to change the name of the programme to Dance for All, or DFA as it is now known. The range of styles now taught at DFA includes Ballet, Spanish, African and contemporary dance.

The success of DFA can only be fully appreciated when one realises that from just 34 students in 1991, there are nowadays well over 1,000 former DFA students working professionally as dancers and/or teachers and choreographers in many different dance styles, either in South Africa or abroad. Reminiscing about his earliest memories of taking over from the late David Poole's earlier work in Nyanga, Philip Boyd – who was then still a principal dancer with the CAPAB Ballet – described to me how he would manage to skip rehearsals on one or two afternoons a week and drive some 15 kilometres to the township of Gugulethu where: "I would have to clear away the desks in one of the local school's classrooms, set up an old reel-to-reel tape machine, and wait to see if any of the children might turn up to my ballet class!"

In those years, the township children were used to living in a noisy, crowded environment and were still totally unfamiliar either with the precise and carefully controlled exercises and steps of classical ballet or, indeed, with the type of classical music Philip was playing on that old reel-to-reel tape machine. "Although most of these children had grown up singing and dancing, it was to the sounds of vibrant African rhythms, miles apart from the disciplined moves of classical ballet. Nevertheless, a few of the most adventurous pupils were game to give my ballet lessons a try and, interestingly, some of them said that they had been attracted by the soothing qualities of the music I was playing."

One of the many reasons for the later, encouraging growth in the number of DFA students – both male and female – had undoubtedly been the spread from those DFA centres located in townships on the outskirts of Cape Town and out into rural areas such as Barrydale, Montagu, McGregor and Bonnievale. The majority of students started dance classes with DFA at the age of six, graduating at the age of about 18 or 19. It is, of course, really important to stress that the DFA's dedicated staff have always taught their students much more than dance. It is precisely the life skills these youngsters acquire at DFA which lead to the gradual growth of each student's personal mental and physical development. In 2012 the DFA Bridging Programme was created as a finishing year for the senior students. By giving these dancers the opportunity of taking part in regular performances, working with various guest choreographers, this Bridging Programme exposes them to all areas of stagecraft in the performing arts and prepares them for future employment in the professional dance world.

Dance for All's illustrious Honorary Life Patron, Archbishop Emeritus Desmond Tutu, in his inaugural address on the occasion of the opening of the DFA's new premises, had said that: "16 years ago, when Philip Boyd had told people in the townships that he wanted to teach them classical ballet, many had thought that he was just a crazy white man!" It had, of course, been precisely by studying ballet that these children were able to gain such a remarkable level of self-discipline. The Archbishop went on jokingly to quip that: "One would think they are from another planet!" A decade later, on the 12th of August 2017, Dance for All presented an entertaining show called *Music a la Carte* at the Artscape Theatre Centre. Included in the printed programme was a special farewell message from Archbishop Tutu to Philip Boyd – for it was on that occasion that Philip Boyd had decided to announce his intended retirement at the end of 2017.

This is an is an excerpt from Archbishop Emeritus Desmond Tutu's warm and appreciative farewell salute to Philip Boyd: "Over all the years that I have watched Dance for All's students leap across the stage, I have always been deeply moved by the joy and energy radiating from every face and in every move of their supple, well-trained bodies. Remember that these are children who live in the townships of Cape Town, with some of the surrounding rural areas being far from idyllic. In fact, it is more likely that they face the daily challenge of poverty and the stress of those crime-ridden environments. Why then would they embrace the stringent demands of formal dance training? And why would it bring them joy? I believe that when Philip Boyd started DFA in 1991, his dream was to offer children a safe environment where they could be engaged in an enjoyable activity that also required discipline and focus. Visionary indeed! All those who have taken DFA classes have, by learning a skill, and more importantly by gaining in self-esteem, been enabled to take the future into their own hands."

With typical foresight, Philip Boyd, the founder and CEO of Dance for All disclosed the fact that, for the past three years, he had been mentoring his appointed successor, the new Artistic Director, Allison Hendricks. In a letter, dated the 21st of August 2017, Philip told me that, after 26 years: "I felt it was time for me to have a new change of direction. This has been a wonderful journey for me personally and professionally, but it is time for a change and the next chapter of my life. I felt that Allison was the right person to take over this very responsible position and she is doing a very good job."

The following are a few of the farewell messages from students to Philip Boyd on his retirement:

Vuyolwethu Nompetsheni: Mr Philip Boyd has been the most supportive person, not only in dance, but on my academic side. He saw the potential in me and steered me in the right direction. I would not have achieved what I am now if it were not for him. I will forever be grateful for his patience and the advice he gave me. Ndiyabulela Philip!

Annie Hendricks: There is so much to say thank you for, I can't explain how grateful I am. You've taught me so much as a person and as a dancer. You are going to be dearly missed. Wherever you end up in life, may you continue to shine and to spread your light.

Mthuthuzeli November: One can try to find words to describe the work you do and have done for many of us, but there just isn't a way to. From a very small town with just dreams you gave me hope and a home, love and support. I am now living my dream because of the work you do. I can never thank you enough.

Lwando Dutyulwa: From the day I started at Dance for All, 11 years ago, I knew that I was stepping into a place of comfort, filled with endless dreams and undying love. Philip and his staff did and still do a wonderful job by running the Dance for

All Programme. Philip, you have inspired me and taught me so much about life. We know that for you running DFA for 26 years hasn't been easy, but you always pushed because you wanted the best for us. Thank you for changing my life for the better and being my mentor. I will forever be grateful. God bless you!

Farnel Smart: With this message I want to wish you all the very best with the next chapter of your life, and also send you many thanks for everything that you have done not just for me, but for each and every dancer who is dancing both here and internationally. You have been a great inspiration to us and a true asset to the World of Dance. I trust that you will continue being the wonderful human being you are, and may this new journey bring you nothing but joy and happiness.

Andisiwe Dyantyi: It was a great journey to be with you. You played a father figure to all of us. You were easily reachable and it was easy to come to you for assistance at any time. You were always the straight talker, but you never intended to hurt anyone. One never felt you were the CEO because you never had the force of a CEO but rather that of a father. You were the best when it came to ballet classes. Your classes will always be in our minds. You were a very fair teacher and made sure we were all looking good.

Hope Nongqongqo: You have been a mentor and a father to me and I am proud to say you have rubbed off onto me so many rich skills, helping me to become a mentor to others, to continue the legacy you have started. *Enkosi Kakhulu Tata Wesizwe!*

Lorraine Ndindwa: It has been a long and beautiful journey with you and the DFA family. It has been 26 years now and you're still the same person I met when I started dancing with you. The time has come now for you to step down; it's sad for us but you deserve to take your retirement. I thank you for the person I am today – you were the father and teacher to us and a grandparent to our kids. I thank you for bringing DANCE into our lives and family. We are now better people through the discipline that you have instilled in us. I wish you all the best in your new chapter and may you stay the sweet and humble person you are. Thank you, Mr Boyd, for everything!

An important milestone in the history of DFA had been the publication, on the 15th of May 2013, of Gillian Warren-Brown's book *Pieces of a Dream: The Story of Dance for All.* The text of this handsome book is illustrated with some seventy images by local and international photographers. The book opens with the story of Hope Nongqongqo, a founder-student who went on to become Outreach Manager for DFA. The growth and development of Dance for All is brought to life through interviews with students, past and present, as well as with Philip Boyd and Company Manager Marlene Carstens. This fascinating book is still available either from DFA or through reputable publishers. The ISBN number is: 978-0-620-56336-9.

★★★

Although I had heard a great deal about the excellent work being done by Dance for All, my first experience of seeing a dance piece choreographed by someone who had been in any way associated with them was when one of the DFA's former part-time teachers (and a particular protégé of David Poole's) called Mzonke Jama came to London in 1994 with The Cape Ballet (as the CAPAB Company were then calling themselves). They staged a ballet by Mzonke as a part of their season at the Sadler's Wells Theatre. Mzonke's ballet was called *Sithandwa* (meaning 'My Beloved') and had originally been commissioned by Veronica Paeper when she succeeded the late David Poole as the Artistic Director of the CAPAB Ballet Company. Although I found that this early attempt at integrating elements of African dance and culture into the work of what was still essentially a European-style ballet company had been quite interesting, I did not really feel that this experiment was really entirely successful.

Born in Cape Town in 1965 and raised in Gugulethu, Mzonke Jama had taken part as a child in various community activities involving acting, dancing and making music. It was when his initial teacher, Desiree Williams, had cast Mzonke in a small part in a ballet she was staging at the Luxurama Theatre that the teenage Mzonke was first spotted by David Poole; he auditioned Mzonke and then arranged for him to follow a one-year orientation programme at UCT. The young man was then awarded the Mary Renault scholarship to enable him to enrol for the three-year full-time course at the University Ballet School, where his tutor in the choreography classes was Jasmine Honoré. There was a special source of empathy between Mzonke and Jasmine because she was herself at that stage embarking on a period of research into some areas of African dance.

Jasmine supported Mzonke in his first attempts at creating a ballet. When he and I first met, a year or two later, he spoke highly of the way she had guided him, saying that "...she never dictated but tried to help me realise my own ideas. I learnt a great deal from her, especially the need to take particular care with the relationship between movement and music." Although he was brought up in an urban environment, Mzonke spent regular holidays with relatives in the Transkei, where he absorbed aspects of rural African culture and attended traditional African rituals.

Then, first at the UCT Ballet School, and later with CAPAB, Mzonke was able to benefit from the opportunity of working in a disciplined, professional environment, enabling him to acquire a sound grounding in ballet technique as well as in certain established methods of theatrical production. Poole now took over from Jasmine as Mzonke Jama's choreographic mentor; this began the process of guiding Mzonke through his first attempts at actually choreographing a piece for the Company.

Following my disappointment with *Sithandwa*, I was all the more delighted when, some months later, I saw a new piece which Mzonke was choreographing for the students at London's Rambert School, where I was then teaching. This was part of the Rambert School's South Africa Project, born as a result of a conversation in 1993 between President Nelson Mandela and Lady Anya Sainsbury. This was later to enable a number of South African students to study at the Rambert School with the support of scholarships from the Lynbury Trust.

One of those students was Theo Ndidnwa, a very talented teenager whom my colleagues and I had taught in 2001, when he was sent to complete his training at the Rambert School. Although still a little 'rough around the edges', Theo had clearly benefitted a great deal from his time with Dance for All where he had acquired the basis of a sound ballet technique and had been carefully mentored by both Philip Boyd and Phyllis Spira. Following a spectacularly successful career of some 28 years with the CAPAB Ballet Company, Phyllis Spira had retired from the stage and had started working full-time with her husband, Philip, in the running of Dance for All. Her hugely beneficial influence on the development of this fine Outreach Programme was to continue until her untimely death.

Born in 1943 and raised and educated in Johannesburg, Phyllis moved to London to complete her training at the Royal Ballet School in 1959. For the next four years she travelled extensively as a soloist with the Royal Ballet Touring Company. However, although her dancing was certainly greatly admired in

Europe, Phyllis very much wanted to dance full-time in South Africa. She returned to Johannesburg in 1964 to dance initially with the newly-established PACT Ballet Company before joining the CAPAB Ballet where she was to spend the next 28 years, and where she was partnered at first by Gary Burne, and later by Eduard Greyling.

In 1984 Phyllis Spira was awarded the rare honour of being granted the title of Prima Ballerina Assoluta. Following an injury in 1988, Phyllis remained involved in the ballet world as the Principal Ballet Mistress of the CAPAB Ballet until 1999 when it was renamed the Cape Town City Ballet Company. For her important services to ballet in South Africa, Spira was awarded the OMSG (Order of Meritorious Service Gold). The Phyllis Spira Trust continues to assist exceptionally talented DFA students in various ways to help them realise their goal of becoming professional dancers, either in South Africa or overseas.

I have particularly fond memories of working with Phyllis Spira in 1971, when David Poole invited me to choreograph two ballets for the CAPAB Ballet, and I was fortunate to have Phyllis dancing leading roles in both *Ritual* and *Venus According.* Yet Phyllis Spira's lasting legacy to her homeland should perhaps be seen to be her wonderful contribution as a teacher and mentor to her students at Dance for All. Some of her influence on DFA can be summed up in a few of the following quotes from Philip Boyd about her interactions with the DFA's senior students, as published in his *Tribute to Phyllis Spira* in the DFA's 20th Celebration Gala brochure: "So many of Phyllie's best qualities live on in DFA and in the students she trained. That some, such as Noluyanda, are giving back to the organisation, is a powerful testimony because that is what DFA is all about – empowering people to empower themselves." "Something Phyllis (and DFA) always stood for is that there's no sense of entitlement – you have to work to get somewhere." "Phyllis always believed that with all the talent we have in South Africa, we have something to celebrate."

To these tributes I would like to add that after Theo Ndindwa had completed his training at the Rambert School in July 2002, he went on to dance professionally for a while with the Phoenix Dance Theatre Company in Leeds. In 2005, he returned to South Africa to found his own Dance Company. Another fine example of how Phyllis Spira and Philip Boyd's mentoring had equipped Theo not only to succeed at gaining employment as a professional dancer in Europe, but to return to South Africa where he boldly founded his own Dance Company – surely proof, if proof were needed, that Dance for All does indeed empower its students to empower themselves!

The following Tributes to Phyllis Spira are a testimony to the love and respect she engendered:

Eduard Greyling – former CAPAB Ballet Principal Dancer: I was indeed fortunate to spend so many years working with Phyllis. Together we played in this imaginary world of dance, laughing, crying, loving, dying – knowing that our purpose was to reach further into the hearts of those needing to escape from everyday realities.

Dame Monica Mason, DBE – the Director of the Royal Ballet at that time: There are some very special people in the world whose passionate commitment to a cause or project enables them to move mountains, to create something out of nothing, to achieve the seemingly impossible, to enrich people's lives in a remarkable way. Phyllis was, without doubt, one of those people.

Noluyanda Mqulwana – student of Phyllis Spira and former InSPIRAtions Dance Company member: Phyllis Spira was a mother to us all; through her tough love she wanted to live to see us succeed, change our lives for the better and inspire us through every means possible.

Dirk Badenhorst – Director of Mzani Productions and CEO of Cape Town International Ballet Competition: In a country that has lost so many dancers to the perceived glamour of foreign careers, Phyllis selflessly set a shining example, shaped standards and gave unstintingly back to the community right here in our own country and for this she will always be remembered with great admiration and love.

Christopher Kindo – renowned choreographer and teacher: How lucky for the DFA dancers to have been trained and mentored by one of the best ballerinas the world has seen. Through them her legacy will live on.

Lady Anya Sainsbury (née Linden) – former Royal Ballet Ballerina: Phyllis Spira filled the role of ballerina so perfectly and gave so much to her country as a performing artist. Later she became a wonderful director and teacher with Philip Boyd. Their work together has given a range of opportunities to young emerging talent and together they have inspired generations of dancers.

Basil Poole – former UCT Ballet soloist and brother of CAPAB Ballet's former Artistic Director, David Poole: If anybody deserved the accolade of Prima Ballerina Assoluta it was my beloved Phyllis. As my brother David said, it was indeed rare for such a talent and personality to come together to create such magic.

Dame Antoinette Siblley, DBE – former Royal Ballet ballerina: Phyllis Spira made a very important contribution to ballet in South Africa; firstly, as a great South African ballerina, and then for her extraordinary work with Dance for All, based in the townships around Cape Town. Her presence will be sorely missed.

Dr Ramphela Ramphele – Dance for All Patron: Phyllis understood the power of the human body as expressed through dance. She also understood the healing impact of dance on young people who had been wounded by humiliation and deprivation. She has left a legacy of healing through the positive energy released on the dance floor.

Pieter-Dirk Uys – satirist: Tonight, many of us will see you here, standing in the wings, wide-eyed and beautiful, watching the future happen, entranced by the young talent in the spotlight – thanks to your inspiration and love. And me, one of those old fans who, long ago, also sat watching you and Gary Burne dazzle us as you did.

Personally, I was particularly moved by something which Hope Nongqongqo, a founder-student and now the DFA's Outreach manager, is reported to have said when Philip Boyd had first shown the students videos of Phyllis dancing in classical ballet roles. Hope had never seen someone dancing as beautifully as that. "I was attracted to her because she was small and I was small. She had big eyes, I had big eyes. I began to get a vision of myself on stage too".

Hope Nongqongqo had initially started attending Dance for All classes at the age of thirteen in the township of Gugulethu. As the Cape Town Outreach Manager, Hope has been in charge of the township programmes in Gugulethu, Nyanga, Langa and Khayelitsha.

The David Poole Trust Fund

Soon after David Poole had died, this Trust Fund was established in his memory. Funds were raised to assist a number of the Ballet for All students to study at the UCT School of Dance. The Trust also paid for those students' ballet shoes and dance togs, plus their transport costs, as well as meeting the funding of trainee teachers. The following are the names of just a few of the many students who were supported by the David Poole Trust either to study at UCT and/or to proceed to one the DFA's Senior Training Programmes, after Ballet for All had changed its name to Dance for All. This exemplifies their former students' wide range of dancing and teaching engagements both in South Africa and overseas:

Luvuyo Bakana: Outreach Programme student. David Poole Trust Scholarship Programme (DFA Senior Training Programme). Jazzart Dance Theatre and freelance dance teacher in Nyanga.

Zandile Constable: Outreach Programme student. David Poole Trust Scholarship Programme (DFA Senior Training Programme) – DFA Youth Company – Alvin Ailey Summer School (USA) – iKapa Dance Theatre.

Nonzuko Damane: Outreach Programme student – David Poole Trust Scholarship Programme (DFA Senior Training Programme) – Scholarship to Wynberg Girls' High School – Bursary from David Poole Trust to attend UCT Ballet School – freelance professional dancer in Spain and Dubai.

Nkosinathi Figlan: Outreach programme student – DFA Junior, then Senior Training Programmes – 2010 Contemporary Ballet Programme – La Rosa Spanish Dance Theatre.

Asanda Mabayi: Outreach Programme student – David Poole Trust Scholarship Programme (DFA Senior Training Programme) – Went on to work as a dance teacher on both of the DFA's Rural Outreach Programmes, in Barrydale and on its Cape Town Outreach Programme.

Noluyanda Mqulwana: Outreach Programme student – David Poole Trust Scholarship Programme (DFA Senior Training Programme) – DFA Youth Company – Cinevox Junior Company (Switzerland) – After performing with the InSPIRAtions Dance Company and the Cape Town City Ballet, Noluyanda became a dance teacher with DFA and coordinator of its Contemporary Ballet Programme.

Zethu Mtati: A founder-student on the Outreach Programme – Trained at the UCT Ballet School, specialising in Spanish dance. Zethu went on to dance professionally with La Rosa Spanish Dance Theatre.

Bathembu Myira: Outreach Programme student – David Poole Trust Scholarship Programme (DFA Senior Training Programme) – Cape Town City Ballet – Ballet Theatre Afrikan – Finalist in *So You Think You Can Dance* 2009 – iKapa Dance Theatre – Performed in Germany in *The Lion King*.

Theo Ndindwa: Outreach Programme student – David Poole Trust bursary to attend the UCT Ballet School – Rambert School of Ballet and Contemporary Dance (UK) – Phoenix Dance Theatre (UK) –DFA Youth Company – Guest dancer with Cape Town City Ballet – Artistic Director of the iKapa Dance Theatre Company.

Lorraine Ndindwa: A founder-student on the Outreach Programme – Bursary from the David Poole Trust to attend the UCT Ballet School – Dance Teacher at BFA – 2009 Dance Teacher at iKapa Dance Theatre Company.

Mbulelo Austin Ndabeni: Outreach Programme student – David Poole Trust Scholarship Programme (DFA Senior Training Programme) – UCT School of Dance – Cape Town City Ballet – Central School of Dance, London.

Nicolette Letube: A founder-student on the Outreach Programme – Jazzart Dance Theatre student training programme – Went on to work in Arts Management.

Mbulelo Ngubombini (Jonas): Outreach Programme student – David Poole Trust Scholarship Programme (DFA Senior Training Programme) – DFA Youth Company – Central School of Dance (UK) UCT School of Dance – Cape Town City Ballet – iKapa Dance Theatre.

Hope Nongqongqo: A founder-student on the Outreach Programme – Bursary from the David Poole Trust to attend the UCT Ballet School – Drummer, Dance Teacher, Choreographer – Co-ordinator of the African Contemporary Programme and of the Outreach Programme.

In the mid-1990s, when Mzonke started working with the Rambert School Students, he began by conducting choreographic workshops in preparation for a ballet called *Imbeleko*, a word relating to the traditional African ritual associated with the naming of a girl child. As I watched Mzonke interacting with our students, I suddenly became aware of the true potential for blending elements of African dance, music and culture with aspects of European-based theatre dance, rooted in ballet and in more modern dance styles. Discussing with Mzonke the differences between his rather artificial-looking ballet *Sithandwa* and his new, fresh and compelling piece *Imbeleko*, which was being so splendidly performed by our young Rambert students, I began to realise why his first ballet had failed and the new one was clearly going to succeed.

According to Mzonke, when Veronica Paeper commissioned *Sithandwa,* she had stressed that he must realise that he would be "…working with a ballet company and should not embarrass the dancers by asking them to perform movements alien to them." With *Imbeleko*, Mzonke had been given a free hand by Ross McKim, the Director of the Rambert School. Firstly, there had been a highly successful initial workshop during which Mzonke and the students had been able to get to know one another. Secondly – and this I feel could have made the fundamental difference – the students at the Rambert School are a very well-integrated group of young people of many different nationalities and racial backgrounds. They also have a thorough grounding in both modern dance and classical ballet techniques and were much more open and receptive to new ideas than the CAPAB dancers would have been when they were working on *Sithandwa*. That was at a time when racial integration was still too recent in South Africa for such an experiment in blending two very different cultural traditions to be able to succeed.

Times have changed and, in many ways, it has been thanks to organisations like Dance for All that things have moved on. Looking back to 1996, I find that I had written the following: "It will take time for a truly multi-racial society to develop in South Africa and, therefore, for multi-cultural art forms to emerge and crystallise; but the potential is enormous." I then tried to analyse the situation as I seemed to see it developing: "African dance and African mythology are rooted in rural societies; but with the ever-increasing move to the cities, there is a need to come to terms with the increasing urbanisation of entire black communities. The philosophy underpinning Mzonke Jama's approach to choreography stemmed from his desire to reflect the essential characteristics of that urban society in his dances, yet without discarding those rural traditions which give his work its identity."

At that time, it certainly seemed to me that it would be precisely out of such an approach that, gradually, a new and recognisably South African style of ballet could possibly emerge. What seemed essential to my way of thinking was that such a style should be allowed to grow and mature slowly and naturally, without forcing the pace, so that what evolved would be something true and organic, and not the result of artificial social engineering. Was I being too unrealistic? And given the fairly recent protests from my old alma mater, the UCT Ballet School, that ballet is "…too Eurocentric and has no place in the new South Africa", should we perhaps not be contemplating the evolution of a 'South African ballet style', but perhaps be thinking more in terms of the emergence of a dance style which truly reflects South Africa's new, multi-cultural society?

Yet, sadly, and in spite of the enormous progress being made by organisations like Dance for All, everything is not entirely harmonious in what was predicted to become "The Rainbow Nation". So perhaps my wanting to see the emergence of a truly multi-cultural society and, with it, genuinely multi-cultural dance styles and other similarly new, truly multi-cultural art forms will, indeed, have to be allowed to develop organically over more than one generation?

To anyone who says that all this seems a long way from what Dulcie Howes was trying to develop, I would say two things. Firstly – and most obviously – that South Africa is now a very different country and a very different society to that which had fostered the University Ballet School and CAPAB. Secondly, I would direct them to an interview which Dulcie Howes gave to *The Star* as long ago as December 1986, in which she stated that: "I want to see the young people dictate, take over. Very often new work spells box-office disaster, but we've got to ride those disasters. We must go on doing it because one is always hoping that some good will come out of it. I don't mean we must write ballets about the mine dumps or the drought in the Orange Free State, but we are under different stresses and strains to other people in the world. The youth are very aware of this and, therefore, it should be reflected in what we are doing if this art is to keep living and is not to become a museum piece."

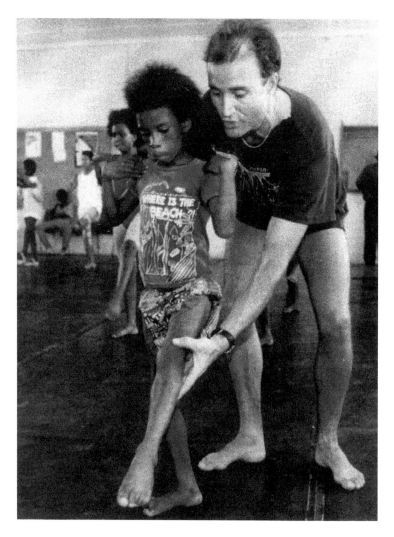

Philip Boyd teaching Nobunto Nqolase in
Gugulethu. *Photo courtesy of DFA*

Phyllis Spira and Eduard Greyling. Stars of the CAPAB Ballet Company.
Photo Keith Mackintosh

Phyllis Spira coaching Nqaba Mafilika. *Photo George Hallet*

Phyllis Spira with little Zintle Ndindwa. *Photo courtesy of DFA*

Lisa Babe in a yellow scarf. *Photo Oscar O'Ryan*

Portrait of a young boy. *Photo courtesy of DFA*

Robin and Bongi in "Comings and Goings".
Photo Pat Bromilow-Downing

Odwa Makanda in a ballet class. *Photo Leonore Cairncross*

Philip Boyd correcting a student in a ballet class.
Photo courtesy of DFA

Farnel Smart and Nathan Bartman. *Photo Pat Bromilow-Downing*

Philip coaching a former male student. *Photo Oscar O'Ryan*

Adrian Abrahams, Stanford Ngamalane, Josephine van den Nieuwendijk
and Tanzley Jooste in a contemporary work.
Photo Oscar O'Ryan

Epilogue

Although this book has dealt specifically with the fact that David Poole's life was blighted by *apartheid*, there were, of course, thousands of other South African citizens of all races whose lives were also blighted in one way or another by the Nationalist Government's harsh *apartheid* legislation.

As we have already seen, as far as the Arts were concerned, the effect of that legislation was either to limit or, indeed, sometimes totally to prohibit musicians, dancers and actors from associating with other like-minded artists. It also determined where and to whom they were allowed to perform, as well as where and with whom they could be allowed to study. In nearly all these cases, Cape Town University's Ballet School, its College of Music and its Michaelis School of Art acted as beacons of light – as did the liberal Cape Town Municipality. That Municipality continued to open its City Hall to all races until the intransigent authorities finally managed to clamp down on just about all such *apartheid* legislative anomalies.

In a totally different sphere, the wrath of the authorities was directed specifically at *political* activists. The National Government did, of course, suffer from a paranoid fear of what, in popular parlance, was often referred to as *Reds under the Beds;* and many – although by no means all – of South Africa's political activists *were* indeed members of the banned Communist Party.

The Congress Alliance was an anti-*apartheid* coalition formed in South Africa in the 1950s. Although it was led by the African National Congress (ANC), the Congress Alliance (CA) was multi-racial in its makeup and was primarily committed to striving peacefully for the establishment of majority rule, something to which South Africa's *apartheid* government was, of course, totally opposed!

In December 1956 many key members of the CA were arrested and charged with treason, including Nelson Mandela and the entire executive committee of the ANC. The racial diversity of the activists arrested included 105 Africans, 21 Indians, 23 whites and 7 coloured members of the CA. About half of the whites arrested were South African Jews. These arrests were to lead to the notorious Treason Trial. The main parts of that Trial lasted until 1961 and, although all the defendants were initially found not guilty, several of them – including Nelson Mandela – were later convicted at the Rivonia Trial in 1964 and were given very harsh and lengthy prison sentences.

The notorious Sharpeville Massacre had taken place on the 21st of March 1960, during which the South African police had fired on a large group of Africans who were protesting against the restrictive pass laws. 69 people were killed, including 8 women and 10 children. Some 180 people were left seriously injured as they were shot in the back, fleeing a hail of police bullets. It was in the wake of this massacre, and with the growing feeling that protestors were being denied all possible peaceful political avenues for change, that the ANC finally decided to form its armed wing, *Umkhonto we Sizwe* ("The Spear of the Nation").

Following the violence and the many bombings that were now going to be perpetrated by the ANC's military wing, many of the political activists who had been able to escape arrest now fled abroad. The vicious manner in which many of them continued to be hunted down by the South African government can be graphically illustrated by the fate of Ruth First.

Ruth First had been one of the defendants in the Treason Trial, alongside 156 leading anti-*apartheid* activists who were key figures in the Congress Alliance. After the state of emergency imposed following the Sharpeville massacre, Ruth First was listed as banned; this meant that she was no longer allowed to attend political meetings, to publish articles, or even to be quoted. In 1963, during another government crackdown, she was imprisoned and held in isolation without charge for 117 days under the Ninety Day Detention legislation – the first woman to be detained under that law.

In March 1964, Ruth First went into exile in London, where she became active in the British Anti-Apartheid Movement. Following a spell as a Research Fellow at the University of Manchester, she lectured in development studies at Durham University until 1978, when she took up the post of director at the Centre of African Studies in Maputo, Mozambique. It was there, on the 17th of August 1982, that Ruth First was assassinated as she opened a parcel concealing a bomb. It had been sent to her by order of a Major in the South African Police Force.

In spite of a series of only partially successful trade boycotts, followed by increasingly stringent academic ones, as well as boycotts by the UK's actors' union, Equity, it was eventually with the imposition of further restrictions on travel to South Africa by several international sporting bodies that the 'sports-mad' South Africans finally began to appreciate the damage being done to their homeland by *apartheid*, compelling them finally to take note of the opprobrium in which South Africa was being held by almost the entire international community.

The part played by the Basil D'Oliveira controversy of 1968 can be seen as a small but important early step on the way to the eventual demise of *apartheid*. A brilliant cricketer and the pride of Cape Town's Cape Coloured community, D'Oliveira was to escape from South Africa early during the *apartheid* era and was eventually to achieve remarkable success playing cricket for England. Basil D'Oliveira's ability to escape the rigours of South Africa's race laws to achieve sporting success in the UK is, in some ways, comparable to David Poole's rise to stardom with the Sadler's Wells Theatre Ballet – but the vexed issue of the tacit 'hierarchy of pigmentation' still then active in South Africa tells a different story.

Poole was sufficiently pale-skinned to enable him to 'pass for White', unlike D'Oliveira, a very slightly darker-skinned Cape Coloured man. Whereas Poole could move freely among the White community, D'Oliveira, before fleeing South Africa, had had to live, work and play his cricket in those areas assigned to the Cape Coloured community in compliance with the relevant race laws. An even more extreme example was that of the very much darker-skinned Johaar Mosaval. Also trained at UCT, Mosaval was enjoying a huge success as a soloist with London's SWTB, but he was not allowed to join David Poole and several of the other genuinely White South African dancers of the SWTB when that Company was invited to perform in their homeland in 1954.

In 1968, South Africa's cricket officials began to realise that if D'Oliveira was to be included in the English squad, it might put future English tours to South Africa in jeopardy. This, in turn, exerted pressure on the MCC, resulting in the controversial decision NOT to pick D'Oliveira for inclusion in future tours to South Africa – not an honourable decision, but a cunning way of keeping cricket links with South Africa open. Indeed, the SA Prime Minister, J B Vorster, had made it quite clear that D'Oliveira's inclusion in the English side would have been unacceptable to South Africa. This led to dissent in the British press. As fate would have it, one of the English players had to be ruled out because of injury, and D'Oliveira was ultimately chosen to replace him. Despite many heated negotiations, the tour had to be cancelled. The D'Oliveira Affair had a huge impact on international opinion against the South African regime, prompting changes in sport in South Africa and, eventually, in society too. (For the definitive account of the D'Oliveira Affair see Peter Osbourne's brilliant book *Basil D'Oliveira* first published by Little, Brown in 2004.)

It was Frederick Willem de Klerk, the 7th and last head of South Africa during the *apartheid* era, who finally helped broker the end of his country's era of racial discrimination and segregation, leading eventually to the release of Nelson Mandela and the long-awaited transformation of South Africa into a non-racial democracy, with equal voting rights for all its citizens.

On a strictly personal note, I feel that, as a white man living, studying and working in South Africa during a large part of the *apartheid* era, there may be a need for me to describe and explain my own reaction to *apartheid*. Together with the vast majority of my fellow-students at Cape Town University, I was appalled by the newly-elected Nationalist Government's promulgation of a series of race laws. Many of us took part in various peaceful anti-*apartheid* protests and – perhaps somewhat naïvely – I imagine we honestly thought that we might be able to get the authorities to change some of their most extreme policies. The Sharpeville massacre certainly disabused us of all such liberal fantasies!

Heather and I were married on the 20th of January 1963 and we had both decided by then to leave Cape Town soon afterwards, with the intention of living in Europe permanently, or at least until there might be a change of government in our homeland. Far from there being any such change, the Nationalist government became more and more intransigent and determined to ignore all international protests and boycotts. In 1971, soon after his appointment to succeed Dulcie Howes as Artistic Director of CAPAB Ballet, David Poole invited me to choreograph two ballets for his Company. Heather and I now had two young children and the temptation to have a paid family holiday with them in Cape Town was difficult to resist. I must leave it to my readers to judge whether accepting to work with a Nationalist government-funded 'white' ballet company, run by someone the authorities certainly knew to be a 'coloured' man was, or was not, the ethical thing to do?

I had started to write this book primarily about David Poole and the effects of *apartheid* on his life. It was only when I was more than halfway through my narrative that my attention was drawn to the ground-breaking work being done in the townships by Philip Boyd and his wife, Phyllis Spira, with Dance for All. That work had been started initially by David Poole, shortly before his untimely death. During several visits to the new, post-Mandela South Africa, I had already become greatly interested in the excellent work Derek Joubert was doing in the Cape-coloured areas of Barrydale with an educational outreach programme called *Net vir Pret* ('Just for Fun'). It was then brought to my attention that Barrydale was also one of the areas served by Dance for All's own rural outreach programme. So, let me end on the happy thought that both Derek and Philip, each in his own way, has taken over the work started by David Poole all those years ago!

Acknowledgements

I could not have written this book without the help and encouragement of Derek Joubert. His intimate understanding of South African society under the *apartheid* regime was an invaluable source of information for me.

Sir Peter Wright and Miss Barbara Fewster OBE were both colleagues and friends of David Poole's during his years with the Sadler's Wells Theatre Ballet and they generously shared their memories of those early days with me.

Marina and Mikael Grut probably knew David Poole better and for longer than any of my other friends and colleagues, whilst Marina's seminal work *The History of Ballet in South Africa* is an absolutely essential reference book on that subject.

Jasmine Honoré's personal knowledge of both the Poole and the Mosaval families was of paramount importance for my understanding of their respective backgrounds. I was also grateful to Dudley Tomlinson for his reminiscences of David Poole's younger brother, Basil.

Keith Mackintosh kindly put me in touch again with Victor Hughes, one of my former students, for whom David Poole was later to become an important mentor.

Philip Boyd, Founder and CEO of Dance for All, has generously shared with me a great deal of the information about that organisation's history and development and I am truly grateful for his help. The generous co-operation of so many of the photographers who have recorded the work of DFA is also warmly acknowledged.

My son, Ben, and my grandson, Ezra Glasstone, were generous with their technological expertise and my wife, Heather Magoon, was, as always, both patient and supportive beyond the call of duty!

When I was writing my biography of Dulcie Howes, her daughters, Amelia and Victoria, generously gave me full access to her private papers. Extracts from these and from personal letters to me are included in this book.

Index by Chapter

Zonova, Cécilée was Cecily Robinson's stage name. For detailed information about Robinson's seminal influence on the development of ballet in Cape Town see Richard Glasstone's autobiography *Congo to Covent Garden*, published by Blurb books.